MW00332851

THE BEST OF
CHELSEA

Jules Gammond

THE BEST OF

CHELSEA

First published in the UK in 2007

Updated and reprinted in 2019

www.G2ent.co.uk

Printed and bound printed in Europe

ISBN 978-1-782816-57-7

Contents

Abramovich

RIGHT Roman's Legionnaires

BELOW Abramovich meets the fans in 2003

Roman Abramovich took control of Chelsea in 2003 and has effectively bank rolled their place in the top tier of English and European football since then winning innumerable prizes in the process.

Born in Saratov, Russia on 24 October 1966 and orphaned at the age of four, Abramovich was brought up by his paternal uncle before being drafted into the Soviet Army.

The collapse of communism and the rapid switch to a free economy enabled Abramovich to acquire vast wealth very quickly as he bought up cheaply shares in the newly-privatised industries and he was soon the major shareholder in Sibneft, the oil company, and RusAl,

the aluminum company.

By 2015 his wealth was estimated at $9 billion (Forbes), making him the one of the richest Russians in the world.

Although he was known to have looked at a number of football clubs in Europe and was believed to have been a fan of CSKA in Moscow, he invested an initial £150 million to buy the controlling interest in Chelsea in 2003. Almost unlimitless funds have been made available since then in order that the club can lure the world's top players to Stamford Bridge, together with a charismatic manager to look after the team. Following accusations that his involvement with Chelsea was unpatriotic, he agreed a £30 million sponsorship deal with CSKA Moscow and Sibneft, thus avoiding UEFA regulations that prevent one person owning more than one club.

Under his patronage Chelsea has won five Premiership titles; five FA Cups; three League Cups; two Europa League Cups and, his ultimate goal, the Champions League Final in 2012.

LEFT Chelsea Chairman, Roman Abramovich watching his team play Leicester In August 2014

ABOVE Carlo Ancelotti celebrating a first League and Cup Double with John Terry

Ancelotti

Carlo Ancelotti was appointed manager of Chelsea in the summer of 2009 and in his first season won both the Premier League and the FA Cup - the club's first ever domestic double.

He succeeded temporary replacement Guus Hiddink and became the club's fifth manager in 21 months, following Jose Mourinho, Avram Grant, Luiz Felipe Scolari and the hugely popular Hiddink. The third Chelsea manager hailing from Italy - after Gianluca Vialli and Claudio Ranieri - he continued with his midas touch at the Bridge.

As a player, "Carletto", as he was nicknamed, appeared 26 times for Italy and participated in the 1986 and 1990 World Cups. A creative midfielder, he started his club career in 1976 with Parma and in 1979 was transferred to AS Roma, where as captain he won the Italian Championship in 1983 and the Italian Cup four times.

From 1987 until 1992 he played for AC Milan and was part of the legendary squad that included the likes of Paolo Maldini and Marco van Basten and won consecutive European Cups in 1989 and 1990.

Ancelotti's first coaching jobs were with Reggiana, Parma and Juventus (where he finished runner-up twice in Serie A) before joining Milan in 2001 where he became one of only six coaches to win the Champions League as both a player and a manager. After his shock departure at Chelsea in 2011(he was greatly loved by fans and players alike) he managed Paris Saint-Germain and Real Madrid where he helped them secure their 10th Champions League Final in 2014 before being sacked at the end of the 2015 season.

Armstrong

LEFT Ken Armstrong shows off his strong arms

Ken Armstrong was spotted whilst playing war-time football with Bradford Rovers and the army before he was signed up by Chelsea in December 1946.

Born in Bradford on 3 June 1924, he made his debut in August 1947 and would go on to make a then record number of appearances for the club, amassing 362 League appearances and 39 appearances in the FA Cup before moving on in 1956.

A member of the side that won the League title for the first time in 1954-55, Armstrong also won one cap for England, a figure that might have been considerably higher had he not been susceptible to injuries.

As it was this solid and reliable right half brought his English career to a halt in 1956 and emigrated to New Zealand, turning out for the likes of Easter Union, New Shore United and Gisborne and winning 13 caps for his adopted country before going into coaching.

He died in New Zealand on 13 June 1984 and his ashes were fittingly scattered at Stamford Bridge.

Azpilicueta

Affectiontaley known as 'Dave' by the fans who can't pronounce his name, there were a few raised eyebrows when Cesar Azpilicueta replaced Ashley Cole at left back as he had been signed from Marseille in August 2012 as a right-back!

But his defensive skills at snuffling opposition wingers meant that Jose Mourinho wanted him in the team even out of position: "Azpilicueta is the kind of player I like a lot. I think a team with eleven Azpilicuetas would probably win the competition (Champions League) because football is not just about pure talent".

His sterling performances for the Blues earned a first call-up to the full Spanish national team in early 2013, and he ended his second season at the club by winning the Chelsea Players' Player of the Year award. He made his 250th Chelsea appearance in the away game at West Ham United in December 2017 and following the departure of Gary Cahill in the summer of 2019, he became the club captain.

Ballack

One of the big name recruits at the start of the Abramovich era was East-German born Michael Ballack who joined the club in May 2006 on a Bosman free transfer.

He began his professional career with Chemnitzer FC and made his reputation with 1FC Kaiserslautern, earning the first of his near 100 caps for Germany in April 1996 and being one of the key players who guided the side to the final of the World Cup in 2002, although he had to sit out the final owing to suspension.

Ballack joined Bayer Leverkusen shortly after his international debut, costing the club 4.8million Euros, and developed into one of the best attacking midfield players in the world, taking Bayer Leverkusen from mid-table obscurity to challenging for honours – in 2001-02 they finished second in the Bundesliga and runners-up in both the German Cup and UEFA Champions League, although Michael received some compensation by being named German Player of the Year.

That year he joined Bayern Munich for 12.9million Euros and started to

OPPOSITE Azpilicueta playing for Chelsea in the 1-0 win against Everton in 2015

ABOVE Ballack signs for Chelsea, May 2006

RIGHT Ballack playing for Chelsea in his typical leisurely fashion in 2008

collect winners medals, winning the Bundesliga at the end of his first season. He also retained his Player of the Year award and, after a trying 2003-04 season, was back in top form the following term and collected the accolade for a third time – only Franz Beckenbauer with four has won the honour more times.

In four seasons at Bayern Munich, he helped the club win three domestic Doubles but his star has failed to shine so brightly at Chelsea. He did help the team win the FA Cup and League Cup in his first season; reach the 2008 Champions League Final; and achieve the League and Cup Double in 2009-10. A technically gifted player who finally won the favour of the fans, he returned to Bayer Leverkusen after some 166 games for the Blues in which he scored 25 goals.

Bates

No football club chairman before or since has aroused quite as much argument both for and against as Ken Bates.

Born in London on 4 December 1931, Ken made his fortune from the ready-mix concrete business and dairy farming before he found an interest in football, briefly serving Oldham as chairman during the 1960s and buying a controlling interest in Wigan in 1981.

The following year he bought Chelsea for £1, inheriting substantial debts, a club languishing in the Second Division and a team clearly not good enough to get them out of trouble. Over the course of the next 20 years Ken rescued the club from bankruptcy, saw off the threat of Marler Estates and turned the ground into one of the best in the country. Along the way he managed to upset all and sundry, failing in an application to electrify the fence surrounding the pitch in order to deter hooligans, welcoming investors such as Matthew Harding into the club and then effectively freezing him out and doing his utmost to deter those he saw as freeloaders. Aided by massive spending both on and off the pitch Chelsea's fortunes were turned around, with the club enjoying sustained success towards the end of the 1990s and emerging at the start of the new century as a major threat to

LEFT Ken Bates generously applauds his team

ABOVE Bates shows Vialli where the exit is, for future reference!

the previous duopoly of Arsenal and Manchester United. By 2003 debts had spiralled back up to £80 million and Ken accepted an offer of £140 million for his controlling interest from Roman Abramovich, although he remained as chairman until March 2004.

Later the same month he announced his intention of investing in Sheffield Wednesday but this deal fell through and in January 2005 he emerged as the new owner of Leeds United. He sold his interest in the club in 2012 and now resides in semi-retirement in Monaco. He may have saved Chelsea from possible extinction but he was involved in too many clubs to win the fans' undying affection.

Bentley

Centre-forward Roy Bentley - one of the last survivors of the title-winning team of 1955 - is up there with the greatest names in Chelsea's long and illustrious history.

He began his career with Bristol Rovers in 1937 but spent only one year on their books before switching across the city to join rivals Bristol City!

Like many players of his era his best years were undoubtedly lost to the Second World War, but at the end of hostilities he moved north to join Newcastle United in June 1946. He was to make 48 League appearances for the Magpies, scoring 22 goals.

In January 1948 Chelsea paid £11,000 to bring him south and, given that he went on to score 149 goals in 366 appearances in league and cup, it must rank as one of the best deals in the club's history. A member of the League championship winning side in 1954-55, Bentley also netted in the following season's Charity Shield.

His Chelsea career came to an end in August 1956 and once again he moved across a city, this time signing for Fulham. The transfer came to £8,500, meaning Chelsea had paid just £2,500 for eight years use out of Bentley, during which he was top scorer in every season.

He later moved into management, taking charge at Reading and Swansea Town. Bentley also proved his worth on the international scene, netting seven goals for England in just a dozen appearances. Following the death of Tom Finney in February 2014, Bentley became the only surviving player from England's 1950 World Cup squad.

BELOW Captain Roy Bentley leads out his Championship-winning team

RIGHT
Frank Blunstone pictured during training at Stamford Bridge in the 1950s

Blunstone

Frank Blunstone was the teenage prodigy of his day. Born in Crewe on 17 October 1934, he joined his local side, Crewe Alexandra straight from school and was thrown almost immediately into the first team in January 1952.

During the course of just 48 appearances for the Railwaymen he was noted as one of the brightest left wing talents in the lower leagues and numerous clubs sent scouts to have him watched.

In March 1953 he was signed by Chelsea for £7,000 and he soon proved that the step up a grade did not phase him, going on to win the first of his five England caps in November 1954 and helping Chelsea win the League championship at the end of the 1954-55 season.

He remained at Stamford Bridge for the rest of his career, finally retiring in June 1964 having helped the club restore their place in the top flight in 1962-63.

In nearly 350 first team appearances for Chelsea he scored over 50 goals, an adequate return for a winger, but it was the goals he created for the likes of Roy Bentley and then Jimmy Greaves that ensured his place in Chelsea folklore.

Bonetti

Peter "The Cat" Bonetti is truly one of the greats from Chelsea's past.

After a brief spell at Reading as a youngster, Bonetti joined Chelsea in April 1959 after his Swiss mother wrote to the club asking for a trial for 'my boy, who might one day make you a useful goalkeeper.' Mrs Bonetti was a master of understatement, for during the course of near on 20 years, Peter made 600 League appearances and 129 appearances in various cup competitions for the Blues keeping more than 200 clean sheets.

Nicknamed The Cat because of his cat-like agility in the penalty area, Bonetti represented England at Under 23 level before collecting his first full cap against Denmark in 1966 and was a member of the squad for the World Cup that year. Unfortunately, the continued good form of Gordon Banks prevented Bonetti from winning more than seven caps for his country, although he did get to represent England in the 1970 World Cup in the quarter-final when Banks had been taken ill with food poisoning. He was largely blamed for their shock defeat to West Germany after they had been leading by two goals although arguably he was only culpable for one of the three goals he let in.

A member of the team that won the FA Cup and European Cup Winners' Cup in successive seasons in the 1970s, and after a brief spell playing in the NASL with St Louis Stars, he finished his career back at Stamford Bridge in 1978 . He returned once more to the Bridge as part of the coaching team and now in his mid-70s still comes back for the occasional guest appearance.

LEFT Peter Bonetti – The Cat

ABOVE Bonetti pictured in 1976

Bumstead

London-born John Bumstead spent his entire playing career in the capital. A Rotherhithe boy, he was fist spotted playing school football in South London before being Invited along to both Queens Park Rangers and Crystal Palace to train. Coveted by both clubs, he decided to join a superior team as an apprentice with Chelsea in November 1976 before joining the professional ranks.

He made his League debut for the club against Leeds United in November 1978 and over the course of nearly 15 years, injuries notwithstanding, would go on to make 339 League appearances and a further 70 in major cup competitions. A midfield creator of goals and chances for others rather than a goalscorer himself, Bumstead still managed to net 38 goals during his Stamford Bridge career.

A member of the side that won the Second Division championship in 1984 and 1989, he was often the unsung hero and highly regarded by his fellow professionals and teammates. In July 1991 he was transferred to Charlton Athletic and went on to make 56 appearances for the club before his retirement.

RIGHT Bumstead keeps a watchful eye on the ball

BELOW John Bumstead in 1983

Cahill

There were a few doubters when Gary Cahill signed for Chelsea in January 2012 from Bolton Wanderers.

The question begged whether he could step up a level. But with John Terry alongside him, the no-nonsense central defender started to read the game better and he was rewarded for his move south with two winners' medals in his first six months in West London, including in his maiden Champions League campaign.

Wearing his favourite 24 shirt, he was a pivotal figure during the 2013-14 season as the Blues kept the best defensive record in the Premier League, and he ended the season being voted into the Premier League's Team of the Season, as well as playing all three of England's matches at the World Cup in Brazil.

By the following May, Cahill had won a Premier League medal and became the fastest player in PL history to win every major trophy available, the FA Cup and UEFA Champions League in 2012, the UEFA Europa League in 2013, and then the Football League Cup and Premier League in 2015, all in the space of three years!

Somewhat harshly frozen out of the first team by obstinate new manager Maurizio Sarri in the 2018/19 season – who never explained why – Cahill joined Crystal Palace for the start of the 2019/20 season after two years as club captain, having played 291 times for the Blues and scoring 25 goals.

LEFT Gary Cahill on his toes in the 2-1 win against QPR in November 2014

Canoville

Paul Canoville holds a paramount place in the history of the club as the first black player to appear in the first team overcoming considerable racial prejudice from fans across the country including from his own supporters!

Canoville ignored the taunts and played more than 100 games in between 1981 and 1986 after signing from non-league Hillingdon Borough. He made his debut as a substitute in a win at Crystal Palace, enduring racist abuse while he was warming up and when he came onto the pitch.

In his second season, one of the worse in the club's history, he made an important contribution to an ultimately successful fight against relegation. He was also a vital member of the squad that won promotion in 1984, while his greatest moment as a Chelsea player came in a League Cup quarter-final in 1985: the team trailed Sheffield Wednesday 3-0 at half-time when he came on as substitute and scored within 11 seconds; and later added another in a memorable 4-4 draw.

His form fluctuated and he joined Reading in 1986 before a serious knee injury prematurely ended his professional career at the age of 24. Since then he has battled drugs, family tragedy, depression and two cancer diagnoses, which nearly cost him his life. He decided to put his triumphs and challenges, on and off of the football field, in print by writing *Black and Blue: How Racism, Drugs and Cancer Almost Destroyed Me* which was highly acclaimed and one of the first to reveal the vitriol and violence that black players had to suffer.

A pioneer and longstanding champion against racism in football, he launched The Paul Canoville Foundation to help disadvantaged young people in the UK and abroad.

Black and Blue
HOW RACISM, DRUGS AND CANCER ALMOST DESTROYED ME
WINNER OF THE BRITISH SPORTS BOOK OF THE YEAR
PAUL CANOVILLE
'THE BEST SPORTS BOOK OF THE YEAR' OBSERVER

RIGHT Black and Blue: How Racism, Drugs and Cancer Almost Destroyed Me - The award winning book by Paul Canoville

Carvalho

Of all the central defensive pairings over the years, Ricardo Carvalho and John Terry is one that springs to mind as one of the best.

They seemed to compliment each other with one covering for the other almost subconsciously, and both hated to lose! While Terry came through the youth team, Carvalho had made a name for himself with FC Porto, helping the club win successive Portuguese League titles in 2002-03 and 2003-04, the UEFA Cup in 2003 and the Champions League in 2004.

Considered one of the key performers within the Porto side, he was one of the first players his former boss Jose Mourinho identified as a necessity for his new-look Chelsea.

It cost Chelsea a reported £20 million to bring the top class defender to Stamford Bridge but the partnership he quickly established with Terry at the heart of the defence meant it was money well spent. At the end of the season he helped Chelsea win the Premiership and League Cup, meaning he won two trophies per season in each of three, having to settle for just the Premiership in 2005-06.

In the summer of 2010, Carvalho rejoined his mentor Mourinho at Real Madrid. During his six years at Chelsea, he played 210 times scoring 11 goals and helped the club to three Premier League titles, two FA Cups and two Carling Cups.His last big club was Monaco where he played nearly 100 games between 2013 and 2017 but he will be fondly remembered by Chelsea fans as a talented ball-playing yet aggressive centre half who out fought and jumped higher than many taller stockier opponents, sometimes with the help of an illicit grab or two!

ABOVE Ricardo Carvalho challenges Robinho of Manchester City

Cech

RIGHT Petr Cech and Arjen Robben celebrate winning the Premiership for the second year running

BELOW Petr Cech and Didier Drogba celebrate winning the Premiership, 2005

Keeper Petr Cech is nothing short of a legend at Chelsea. He is the club's all-time record clean sheet holder and has also played more games than any other foreign player in the history of the club. Born in the Czech Republic on 20 May 1982, he arrived at Stamford Bridge aged 22 in 2004 for a £10.3 million fee from French club Stade Rennais, with the task of challenging established number one Carlo Cudicini.

At six foot four inches tall, he immediately caught the eye with his incredible reaction speed and positivity in collecting crosses and began his Chelsea career as Jose Mourinho's first choice.

In the dozen years since then he has lifted every major club honour during an extraordinary career in West London. Cech has won four league titles, recovered from a life-threatening injury and saved decisive penalties in both an FA Cup and Champions League final. Add to that an extensive number of personal records, including one for most clean sheets in an English top-flight season, and he is undoubtedly one of the all-time Chelsea greats.

He is also one of the most recognisable players in the team as he has worn a black protective head-cap for the past few years following a dreadful collision with Reading's Stephen Hunt in which he fractured his skull.

ABOVE Cech wearing his protective head guard after he fractured his skull playing for Chelsea

After 494 games for Chelsea – and 13 major trophies - he raised a few eyebrows by joining London rivals Arsenal to play out his final years. But there was no keeping him away from his spiritual home and after retiring in the summer of 2019 he came back as technical and performance advisor alongside of his old team-mate Frank Lampard as manager.

Centenary 1905-2005

With a choice of three dates to chose from (14 March 1905, when the club was founded at The Rising Sun public house, now the Butcher's Hook; 29 May, when the club was elected to the Second Division of the Football League; or 2 September, when the club played its first match away at Stockport County) in which to honour its centenary there were assorted functions and events planned to help the club celebrate.

The first of these was a party thrown at the Butcher's Hook on 14 March 2005, exactly one hundred years since the club was founded at the same venue.

Players from the club's illustrious past including members of the 1955 championship winning side, the 1970 FA Cup winners and more recent stars, joined the then manager Jose Mourinho (although none of the first team squad was permitted to attend as they had an important match the following day) and other dignitaries in celebrating the first planned event.

On 29 May 2005 the club hosted a Centenary Gala Dinner at the Royal Opera House to commemorate their election to the Football League, with the team being allowed to attend this event!

The whole of the 2005-06 season was marked as a centenary season with a special badge appearing on the players' shirts throughout the campaign.

Throughout its history Chelsea has only ever had one home ground, Stamford Bridge, where they have played since their foundation.

ABOVE Football League Champions Chelsea, in 1955

RIGHT Asier Del Horno displays the 2005-06 centenary shirt

Chelsea FC Women

Originally called Chelsea Ladies Football Club, it was founded in 1992 and has been affiliated with Chelsea Football Club since 2004. The first team competes in the FA Women's Super League (with the Reserves playing in the FA WSL Development League Southern Division) and have their own ground at Kingsmeadow, Norbiton, which the club bought off of AFC Wimbledon at the start of the 2017/18 season.

Within two years of forming, the team had won its first honour and like their male counterparts have been challenging the very best sides in the country ever since. New players are nurtured through the Female Centre of Excellence and Academy College Programme while high-quality players with international experience are always on the radar.

In 2015, Chelsea FC Women won a famous double, becoming champions of the FA Women's Super League for the first time and winning the FA Women's Cup at Wembley Stadium. The Blues then followed this up by lifting the FA WSL Spring Series in 2017, and further silverware followed in 2018 with another FA Women's Cup triumph followed by the WSL title, so completing the domestic Double for a second time. Chelsea FC Women also reached the Champions League semi-finals for the first time in their history.

BELOW LEFT Chelsea players celebrating winning the 2014–15 FA Women's Cup

BELOW Katie Chapman current captain of Chelsea FC Women 2015

INSET Assistant manager Steve Clarke

ABOVE Skipper Steve Clarke

Clarke

Steve Clarke served Chelsea admirably well both on and off the pitch.

Born in Saltcoats on 29 August 1963, he arrived at Chelsea a full Scottish international, having won eight caps for his country during his time at St Mirren.

He joined Chelsea in January 1987 and went on to make 330 league appearances for the club, scoring seven goals. A member of the side that won the FA Cup and European Cup Winners' Cup in successive seasons (1996-97 and 1997-98) Steve made more than 400 appearances in total for Chelsea.

At the end of his playing career Steve turned to coaching and was one of Jose Mourinho's first appointments as assistant manager in the summer of 2004.

His coaching prowess earned him positions at Newcastle United, West Ham United, Liverpool and manager roles at West Bromwich Albion, Reading and Kilmarnock, the club he supported as a child and took to a third-placed finish and European qualification at the end of the 2018/19 season. This unprecedented success resulted in him being appointed the Scottish national team manager in May 2019.

Cole

Love him or loathe him, there was little doubt that Ashley Cole was one of the best left backs this country has ever produced.

After playing more than 200 games for Arsenal, his £5m move to Chelsea in

ABOVE Ashley Cole playing in the 2012 Champions League Final

2006 was always going to be a baptism of fire - especially a fans' favourite William Gallas went the other way at the same time. But after shaking off a worrisome ankle injury, he started to show his undoubted class and it was soon forgotten that he was once a Gooner.

He played under five managers at Chelsea, winning the Premier League in the 2009-10 season, four FA Cups (he has won seven in total, more than any other player in history), one Football League Cup and one Champions League trophy in 2012. He finally ended his time at the Bridge after 338 games, and seven goals, in May 2014, when it was obvious that Azpilicueta was going to be first-choice left back and he moved abroad to top Italian side Roma.

In his twilight years he played in the States for LA Galaxy and had one final swansong in the English football league with Derby County (when his old Chelsea colleague Frank Lampard was manager). He won 107 caps for England, making him the country's most capped left back if not the most liked.

LEFT Ashley Cole beating Kolo Toure of Arsenal to the ball

ABOVE Joe Cole being surrounded by West Brom players

Cole

He's here, he's there, he's every ******* where … Joey Cole, Joey Cole. This unprintable homage from the Chelsea faithful, was the theme tune to Joe Cole's near 300 appearances for the club where he played the best football of his career.

Hailed as a child prodigy, he was just 22 when he came to the Bridge in a £7m deal as a product of the West Ham Academy, following in the footsteps of Frank Lampard who made the same transition.

Over the next 18 months or so he

Cup and retained the League title a year later.

At his tantalising best, he was one of the few top players who could get fans out of their seat when he had the ball as there was a touch of genius about his close control and eye for a pass or shot. At Chelsea, he amassed a haul of three Premier League titles, three FA Cups and two Football League Cups but sustained a bad knee injury that kept him out of the second half of the 2008-09 season and he never seemed to have the same zip afterwards.

He joined Liverpool in 2010 (where he failed to connect with the fans) and brought the curtain down on his playing career at West Ham, Aston Villa, Lille, Coventry and Tampa Bay Rowdies. His Chelsea career came full circle when he came back to the club as a coach in the summer of 2019 under the managership of old team-mate Frank Lampard.

ABOVE Joe Cole fighting to keep the ball

struggled to hold down a regular place in the side but under the influence of Jose Mourinho he gradually cut out the sometimes selfish play to work on his all-round contribution and eventually became an integral part of the side that won the FA Premiership and League

Conte

Having led Juventus to three Serie A titles in a row, former Italian international Antonio Conte was appointed manager of Chelsea in the summer of 2016 and proved to be an inspirational choice and not just for his film star looks.

After an inauspicious start with comprehensive defeats against Liverpool and Arsenal in September 2016, Conte adopted a revolutionary 3-4-3 formation that immediately flourished.

The fans loved seeing wide midfielders and wing backs – usually Victor Moses and Marcos Alonso – bombing up and down the wings when the team had the ball; while his system employed two defensive-minded midfielders in N'Golo Kante and Nemanja Matic who protected the back three of David Luiz, Cesar Azpilicueta and Gary Cahill.

He was also blessed with an inspired Diego Costa as his bullish centre forward crucially assisted by the dribbling wizardry of Eden Hazard complimented by Pedro or Willian. It was a heady combination and when the team scored, Conte added to the celebratory frenzy by diving headlong into the arms of the fans.

Chelsea's performances improved dramatically after this tactical change, with 13 consecutive wins in the Premier League, and the team went on to win the league title in his first season - setting a new record for the most wins in a single season, with 30 league victories out of 38 league matches.

He won the Premier League and LMA Manager of the Season Awards and spawned a best-selling book King Conte to mark his sensational start to his career in England.

But the following season, his demeanour gradually ebbed as some of the star players were at loggerheads with his tactical formations – most notably Costa and Hazard – and despite winning a rather dull FA Cup Final with a 1-0 win over arch rivals Manchester United (managed by Jose Mourinho) the team finished fifth in the Premier League, missing out on Champions League qualification.

For Chelsea, this was unacceptable and Conte was dismissed as manager in July 2018 although you always felt that he wanted away to. He is now back managing in Italy at Inter Milan.

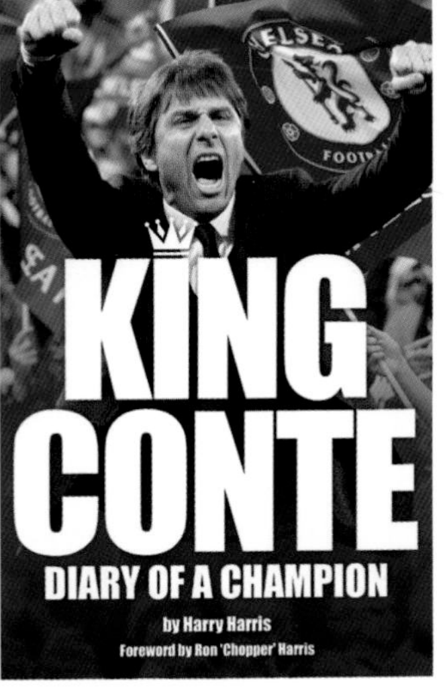

ABOVE The best-selling book King Conte

Cooke

If Eden Hazard had played for Chelsea fifty years ago, he would be closest in style and skill to Charlie Cooke.

Like Eden, 'Charlie' had the dribbling ability to leave defenders on their backsides and, alongside Zola, was one the most skilful and best-loved footballers ever to play for Chelsea.

Signed from Dundee in 1966 as a replacement for Terry Venables, Cooke made his debut in the Fairs Cup semi-final against Barcelona. He had to wait until August to make his league debut during which he easily embarrassed England's World Cup winning centre-half Bobby Moore in scoring the winner against West Ham.

After consecutive FA Cup semi-final defeats prior to his arrival, Chelsea finally won in 1967 making the final for the first time since 1915, and Charlie, the darling of the terraces, was widely recognised as being the reason they made it.

Over the next six seasons Cooke entertained the Chelsea faithful with his extravagant skills and he was a crucial part of the 1970 and 1971 cup-winning teams. His dribble and cross to set up Peter Osgood's late equaliser in the FA Cup Final will forever remain part of Chelsea folklore.

RIGHT Cooke enters the pitch, 1974

BELOW Charlie Cooke pictured in 1974

Cooke was surprisingly allowed to join Crystal Palace in 1972 but returned 18 months later. He was unable to help prevent relegation in 1975 but two years later played a part in supporting a young team win promotion. The Scottish international made a handful of appearances over the next two seasons, making his 373rd and final Chelsea appearance in a memorable FA Cup win over Liverpool.

In the summer of 1978, Cooke moved to the United States where he played for several clubs before retiring. He now runs a Coerver soccer school in Ohio.

LEFT Diego Costa in 'Don't Mess With Me' mode

Costa

Diego Costa's fiery temperament endeared him to the Chelsea faithful who saw a player who wasn't going to be intimidated by the opposing centre half yet also had a skilful first touch and an eye for a goal.

Here was a proper replacement for Drogba and for a couple of seasons – in which he helped the club win two Premier League titles and a League Cup – he was a hero with villainous tendencies who liked to pick a fight with anyone getting in his way.

Born in Brazil, he made a name for himself as a goal scorer in Spain (for whom he played for at international level) helping Atletico Madrid win a La Liga title, a Copa Del Ray title and a UEFA Super Cup.

In his final season he scored more than a goal a game, and the big Premier League clubs came sniffing particularly as his bludgeoning style suited the English game. He arrived from Atletico Madrid on July 15 2014 and got his Chelsea career off to a flyer netting nine goals in his first seven league outings.

His time at Chelsea was peppered with as many skirmishes as goals, with the Daily Express labelling him the 'dirtiest player in the league'. After a while, his petulance started to annoy both the management and fans as it began to be detrimental to the success of the team.

While he helped win a Premier League title under Conte, he was harshly told by text message that he was not part of the manager's plans for the upcoming 2018/19 season. He re-joined Atletico in the January transfer window of 2018. Within a month he had been sent off but ended the season with a Europa League trophy. Wherever he goes, you are only ever going to get the rough with the smooth.

RIGHT Thibaut Courtois one of the top three goalkeepers in the world celebrating winning the Football League Cup with Petr Cech in 2015

Courtois

Fans had an inkling of what they were going to get when giant Belgian keeper Thibaut Courtois - who was signed to Chelsea on a five-year contract in July 2011 - was loaned to Atletico Madrid for the 2011-12 season where he helped his team win the Europa League Cup.

The loan was extended for a further 12 months to cover the 2012-13 season, and Courtois once again impressed. He remained at Atletico for the 2013-14 campaign and finished it as part of a side who had overcome the might of both Barcelona and Real Madrid to win the Spanish title. Atletico also reached the Champions League final but were beaten by Real after extra-time. Only Petr Cech was less than delighted as he feared that his first team place was in danger!

His fears were founded when Mourinho decided to make the 23 year-old his first choice keeper and the agile six foot six inch stopper didn't disappoint. In 39 matches, he kept 15 clean sheets and helped Chelsea win the Premier League title. Two years later he won the Premier League Golden Glove as the Blues again won the league.

He played more than 150 games for Chelsea and was a popular figure with fans until he pushed for a move to Real Madrid signing for £35 million and becoming La Liga's most expensive goalkeeper.

Cudicini

Italian keeper Carlo Cudicini could have walked in to most Premiership teams so it was extremely unfortunate that for a large part of his nine years with Chelsea as understudy to Petr Cech, one of the best goalkeepers in the world.

Born in Milan on 6 September 1973, Carlo followed his father Fabio in signing with AC Milan as a youngster and made two appearances in the Champions League without having made a Serie A appearance. An injury-ridden career was going nowhere at lowly Italian clubs before Chelsea manager Gianluca Vialli required cover for Ed de Goey and had heard good reports of Cudicini prompting a year loan spell that subsequently became permanent.

The handsome handler eventually made the goalkeeping berth his own and was voted Player of the Year in 2001-02. Injuries continued to plague his career and when Petr Cech arrived during the summer of 2004 he was relegated to second choice keeper.

He still kept 101 clean sheets in 216 appearances for the club, behind only Peter Bonetti and Cech, but the promise of regular first-team football eventually prompted his move to Spurs in January 2009. After playing in the States before retiring, he is now back at his beloved Bridge as part of the coaching staff under Frank Lampard as well a club ambassador.

BELOW Carlo has his hands safely on the ball

Cult Heroes

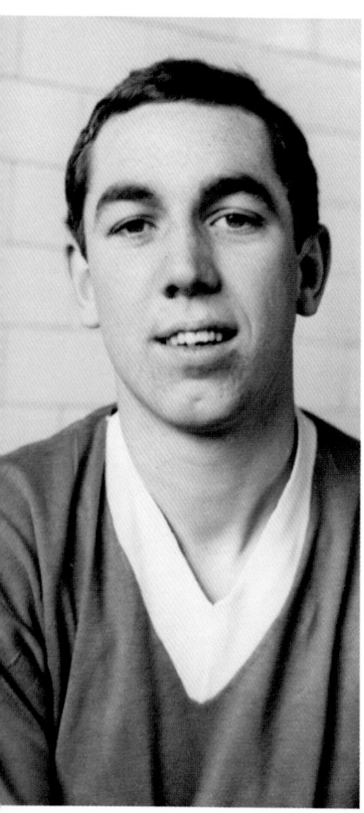

ABOVE Marvellous Marvin Hinton

Every club has them, the players who give everything for the shirt and are idolised by the fans on the terraces.

They tend to fall into two categories. Those that are triers but not supremely skilful ; and those that only played a season or two but are fondly remembered as great players in their short time at the club.

The workhorses at Chelsea have included the likes of Tommy Baldwin, Petar Borota, Ian Britton, Jason Cundy, Mike Fillery, John Dempsey, Tony Dorigo, Mickey Droy, Paul Elliott, Ian Hutchinson, Marvin Hinton, Peter Houseman, Erland Johnsen, Joey Jones, Tommy Langley, Gary Locke, Ken Monkou, Eddie Niedzwiecki, Graham Roberts and Nigel Spackman (who inexplicably has an entrance at the club named after him) but could possibly be epitomised by full-back Dan Petrescu. A fans favourite, he made 208 appearances and scored 23 goals between 1995-2000: 'My memories are only fantastic from Chelsea after five years there, winning so many trophies, being with great players and fantastic fans. I have a daughter who is named Chelsea. It was everything for me. It was the best time in my life as a football player, this is for sure.'

The superstars who shone brightly at the Bridge but not for very long include the likes of super-sub Tore Andre Flo, who scored 50 goals in 163 games; Hernan Crespo who had two spells at Chelsea and won a league title in 2006; Mark Hughes, who was a legend at Manchester United but also played 123 games for Chelsea (winning player of the year in 1997) scoring 39 goals; and Jimmy Floyd Hasselbaink, who in 177 games for Chelsea scored 88 goals most of them pile-drivers from outside the box.

And there are also players who are remembered as bad boys, none more so that Adrian Mutu who scored four goals in his first three matches (two against arch rivals Spurs) but failed a drugs test for cocaine in September 2004 and never enjoyed the highs of Chelsea again.

Desailly

Nicknamed "The Rock", Marcel Desailly was considered one of the most accomplished players of his generation, and one of the finest French defenders, who stood out for his leadership throughout his career.

Born in Accra, Ghana on 7 September 1968, he moved to France whilst still a young child when he was adopted by a French diplomat. An early aptitude towards football saw him signed by FC Nantes in 1986.

Six years and 164 League appearances in defence of Nantes later he was signed by Olympique de Marseille and at the end of his first season with the club had helped them win the UEFA Champions League (the first season under its new format) against AC Milan.

Marseille were subsequently stripped of their title, although Marcel's performances had registered with AC

ABOVE "The Rock", Marcel Desailly

ABOVE LEFT Marcel Desailly battles with Paolo Di Canio

ABOVE RIGHT Marcel Desailly thwarts Luis Boa Morte

Milan, for they signed him midway through the season and he finished 1993-94 helping his new club make up for the previous year's disappointment by winning the UEFA Champions League 4-0 against Barcelona.

Desailly thus became the first player to collect winners medals in consecutive seasons with different clubs.

After helping AC Milan to two domestic League titles during his time with the club, he left in the summer of 1998 to join Chelsea and added to his medal tally with an FA Cup winners' medal in 2000.

A stylish, unhurried performer, Desailly made 158 appearances for the Blues and was highly regarded by both the fans and his team-mates. Although he began his career in defence, such was his ability he could play equally well in midfield. Jody Morris who played alongside him commented: "Maybe at Chelsea they weren't his greatest years but you could still see in the top games he just went into fifth gear."

The winner of 116 French caps (67 of these were collected whilst he was a Chelsea player, making him the club's most capped overseas player), he collected winners medals in both the World Cup (1998) and European Championships (2000) for his adopted country.

The summer of 2004 saw him draw a close to both his international career and his time at Stamford Bridge, subsequently moving on to Qatar to play for Al Gharafa. Now retired, The Rock is settled in Ghana.

Di Matteo

There are a select band of people who both played and managed at Chelsea - Tommy Docherty, Eddie McCreadie, John Hollins, Ruud Gullit - but none can claim to have the same success as Roberto di Matteo.

As a creative midfield player, his passing ability and accurate long-distance shooting saw him become one of the driving forces of Chelsea's resurgence in the late 1990s. He contributed nine goals in his first season, and helped the club finish sixth place in the league, and reach the 1997 FA Cup Final at Wembley. Within 42 seconds of the kick-off against Middlesbrough, Di Matteo scored the opening goal from 30 yards and Chelsea won 2–0.

The following season Di Matteo again proved his worth to the team, contributing ten goals and numerous assists, as Chelsea went on to claim the Football League Cup and the Cup Winners Cup, their first European honour since 1971. In the League Cup final, again against Middlesbrough, Di Matteo scored the second goal in a 2–0 win.

During the 1999-2000 season, Di Matteo was sidelined by injury but returned late in the season to score a handful of crucial goals, including his third Cup-winning goal at Wembley, once again in the FA Cup. In a dour match, Di Matteo capitalised on an error by Aston Villa keeper David James to score the winner in the 71st minute, handing Chelsea their fourth major trophy in three years. This lead Di Matteo to comment on the old Wembley Stadium saying "It's a shame they're tearing the old place down it has been a very lucky ground for me"

Early into the 2000-01 season, Di Matteo sustained a triple leg fracture and did not play for the next 18 months. He gave up on hopes of returning from this injury in February 2002 and retired at the age of 31. In his six years at Chelsea, Di Matteo made 175 appearances and scored 26 goals.

But his crowning glory was yet to come. After taking over the managership from the disastrous Andre Villas Boas, he managed to win the club two major trophies in just eight months in charge. The first of these was the FA Cup Final against Liverpool in May 2012 which he followed by a stunning victory in the Champions League Final defeating Bayern Munch in their own Allianz Arena. The match had ended 1–1 after extra time with Chelsea coming out victorious in the penalty shootout, Drogba scoring the winning spot kick.

This was Chelsea's first Champions League title after the disappointment of Moscow 2008 and no matter what happens to Di Matteo, for the rest of his life he will always be remembered as 'the greatest caretaker manager of all time.'

ABOVE Di Mateo, manager of Chelsea when they won the 2012 Champions League

ABOVE Kerry scores again

Dixon

Kerry Dixon, Chelsea's third highest goal scorer, was nearly lost to professional football.

Born in Luton on 24 July 1961, Dixon was on the books of Spurs as an apprentice but failed to make the grade at White Hart Lane, subsequently slipping out of League football and joining Dunstable Town.

He netted 52 goals in a year and had League clubs taking an interest again, joining Reading in July 1980 for £20,000 and soon establishing himself as a prolific goalscorer. In August 1983 Chelsea paid £175,000 to bring him to Stamford Bridge and he established an understanding with fellow striker David Speedie, netting 28 goals as the club won the Second Division championship in 1983-84.

Dixon continued to score goals in the top flight, finishing his first season as the division's top scorer and prompting calls for an England call-up, which were finally answered when he appeared against Mexico in 1985.

Dixon continued to score goals for Chelsea until July 1992 when having lost his place to Tony Cascarino, he was sold to Southampton for £575,000, having netted 147 League goals in 335 appearances for The Blues. His total tally of 193 goals for Chelsea puts him in third place in the list of all time goalscorers for The Blues, just nine behind Bobby Tambling and 18 behind Frank Lampard.

He didn't settle at The Dell, making just nine appearances and after a spell on loan at Luton made the deal permanent in February 1993.

Dixon, who won eight caps for England, later had spells at Millwall, Watford and Doncaster Rovers, where he was briefly player-manager, before returning to the non-League game with Dunstable.

Although his time at Chelsea was barren trophy wise (apart from two Second Division championships), his goals helped re-establish the club amongst the elite in English football.

ABOVE A youthful Kerry Dixon

LEFT Kerry gold

Docherty

Not many people know it but Tommy Docherty played four games for Chelsea before he made his name as manager in the Swinging Sixties.

A tough-tackling wing half in his playing days, he earned his reputation with Preston North End, joining the club in 1949 from Celtic. The highlight of his career was a runners-up medal in the 1954 FA Cup Final, despite leading at one stage, and after 324 appearances for the Deepdale club, Docherty moved to Arsenal in 1958.

He was with the Gunners for three years, making 83 appearances before his switch to Stamford Bridge in September 1961. Five months later he was appointed manager after Ted Drake's departure, but despite the change Chelsea still ended the season relegated from the First Division.

Docherty re-organised the club and took them back up at the first time of asking and, once returned to the top

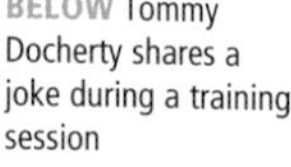

BELOW Tommy Docherty shares a joke during a training session

flight set about turning them into a force to be reckoned with.

He introduced the likes of Terry Venables, Charlie Cooke and Peter Osgood to the side, led them to victory in the 1965 League Cup and stood on the brink of leading them to greatness. Unfortunately, Docherty never got the chance to do so, for he removed from the club those who he felt might undermine his position, including Terry Venables, rowed with the board and managed to lead the club to the 1967 FA Cup Final with most of his players in mutinous mood over bonuses and ticket allocations – they lost to Spurs, with Terry Venables a key component for the opposition.

The ill-feeling generated by the cup run, in particular between Docherty and chairman Charles Pratt simmered on until October 1967 when Docherty resigned.

He subsequently managed myriad clubs including Rotherham, Queens Park Rangers, Manchester United, Derby County and countless others (Docherty claims to have had more clubs than Jack Nicklaus) before ending his managerial career at Altrincham in 1988. Aged 87, he has now all but stopped his media work and after-dinner speaking.

LEFT Plaster on chin, Tommy Docherty still manages a smile

ABOVE Chelsea manager, and proud Scot, Tommy Docherty seems surprisingly pleased that his team are using the coach that carried England to and from matches during their successful World Cup campaign, while Chelsea's Ron Harris looks less sure of its qualities

ABOVE Drogba celebrates scoring his second goal for Chelsea in the 2005 FA Community Shield

Drogba

Having been sent off in the Champions League Final in Moscow 2008, Didier Drogba more than made up for this by scoring the equaliser in the 2012 Final against Bayern Munich and slotting home the winning penalty after extra-time - giving the club the single greatest moment in its history.

He is quite rightly considered as a legend by fans for his crucial final-winning goals and for the way that he led the front line over numerous glorious seasons. They have even forgotten that his propensity to fall over at the slightest touch was considered by many to be cheating.

Drogba first signed for Chelsea for £24 million from Marseille in the summer of 2004, when he was a big man with a growing reputation. He left eight years later a club legend, and returned to Stamford Bridge in July 2014 to work again with Jose Mourinho, the man who had first brought the Ivorian to Stamford Bridge some ten years earlier.

Physically a match for any defender and able to score any type of goal, his ability to take on the opposition back-line single-handed marked Drogba down as one of the finest strikers in the world for many seasons.

Big-game goals were the particular hallmark of the imposing striker's repertoire, and he became the only player in history to score in four separate FA Cup finals when he scored in Chelsea's 2-1 win over Liverpool in the 2012.

He finally called time on his Chelsea career at the end of the 2014-15 season after four Premier League titles, four FA Cups, three Football League Cups and the Champions League in which he scored an incredible 88th minute headed equaliser and the winning penalty in the shoot-out with Bayern Munich in 2012. For that match alone, he will always be considered a club legend.

BELOW Didier Drogba celebrates with the fans after scoring the winning penalty in the 2012 Champions League Final

Essien

RIGHT Michael Essien getting to the ball first

In August 2005, Lyon and Chelsea agreed a £24.4 million fee for Michael Essien, finally ending one of the longest-running transfer sagas in the history of the club.

At the time, the fee made the Ghanaian Chelsea's most expensive signing and he went on to have stalwart career at the club as a holding midfielder weighing in with the odd spectacular goal – none better than his volley against Barcelona in the home leg of the Champions League semi-final.

Chelsea fans voted Essien as Player of the Year for his contributions in the 2006-07 season becoming the first African to receive the honour. His late dramatic equaliser against Arsenal was also voted as Chelsea Goal of the Season for 2006-07.

The "Bison", as he was called by team-mates, made more than 250 appearances for the Blues winning two Premier Leagues, four FA Cups, one League Cup and the Champions League. He rejoined Mourinho on a season-long loan at Real Madrid in 2012 scoring on his last ever match for the club which he dedicated to his mentor. He went on to play for Milan and dropped down various leagues and standards as he reached his mid 30s and looked towards a career in coaching.

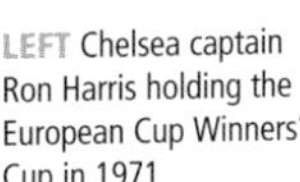

LEFT Chelsea captain Ron Harris holding the European Cup Winners' Cup in 1971

Europe

But for an untimely slip by skipper John Terry in the penalty shoot-out against Manchester United at the 2008 Champions League Final in Moscow, Chelsea would have won the ultimate European trophy four years earlier than they eventually did.

His shot hit the outside of the post instead of flicking in off of the inside; while Didier Drogba's extra-time penalty was driven home to the right side of the goal giving the Blues an incredible victory over Bayern Munich in their own back yard.

Chelsea's European trophy cabinet at last contained the biggest prize of them all. Previously their only notable triumphs had come in the 1971 and 1998 European Cup Winners' Cups.

The first time the club won this competition was against the mighty Real Madrid who had already got six European Cups in their cabinet. The Final went to a replay after a 1-1 draw with Chelsea hanging on to a 2-1 win with goals from

Dempsey and Osgood, to claim the club's first-ever European trophy.

The Cup Winners' Cup 1-0 win in 1998 against VfB Stuttgart was achieved with just 20 minutes remaining through a wonder goal from Gianfranco Zola – 30 seconds after he came off of the bench. The stunning half-volley was the catalyst of the love affair between Zola and Chelsea fans who voted him the club's greatest-ever player.

For years Chelsea have been associated with a whole range of famous people who have supported the Blues. The height of celebrity fandom came during the 'glory years' around the late sixties and early seventies when the style and glamour of the team was matched by those wandering the Kings Road. Chelsea has since won the Europa League twice latterly a 4-1 thrashing of Arsenal in the 2019 Final which saw Eden Hazard score twice and win the man-of-the-match award in his last match for the club. This victory saw them face Liverpool in 2019 UEFA Super Cup in August 2019, which they lost on penalties when Tammy Abraham fluffed his spot kick.

ABOVE Gianluca Vialli holds the trophy aloft after the 1998 European Cup Winners' Cup Final against VfB Stuttgart

ABOVE RIGHT Chelsea players holding aloft the Champions League trophy in 2012

Fabregas

LEFT Cesc Fabregas playing for Chelsea in a league match against Southampton in 2015

If Cesc Fabregas had any doubts over signing for Chelsea in the summer of 2014 after he was spurned by his former club Arsenal, they were dispelled at the end of his first season when he had won his first Premier League title as well as the Football League Cup.

Under Arsène Wenger he might have continued to enhance his reputation as one of Europe's most creative midfield players but he wouldn't have had a sniff of the league title.

Fàbregas started his career as a trainee with Barcelona before he was signed by Arsenal in September 2003 at the age of 16. Following injuries to key midfielders in the 2004-05 season, he made the central midfield position his own and became the team's playmaker and captain.

He played more than 300 games for the North London club, scoring over

RIGHT Fabregas in action against Karl Henry in the 2-1 win over QPR in November 2014

50 goals, so it was a bit of a shock when he returned to the Catalan giants for a £30 million fee in August 2011.

Despite competition from his international teammates Xavi and Iniesta he tasted regular success in his three seasons at Barcelona, and won the first league title of his career in 2013. When Mourinho heard that the club was willing to let him go, he swooped to sign him for for Chelsea in June 2014, for a £30million fee, after Arsenal had declined to take up their first option to buy him back.

The Gunners loss was Chelsea's gain as in his first year he helped the club win the League Cup and the Premier League. He played some 150 games for Chelsea but fell out of favour with manager Maurizio Sarri and moved to Monaco in January 2019.

Famous Fans

Politics

Lord Sebastian Coe	Ex-MP/Athlete
Tony Banks	Ex-MP (Died 2006)
Sir John Major	Ex-PM
Peter Hain	MP
Peter Bottomley	MP
Ed Vaizey	MP
David Mellor	Ex-MP
Bill Clinton	Ex-President, USA

(watched Chelsea in the 60s)

Sport

Sir Steve Redgrave	Olympic Rower
Jimmy White	Snooker
Tony Drago	Snooker
Sir Clive Woodward	Rugby (England)
Laurence Dallaglio	Rugby (England)
Brian Moore	Rugby (England)
Ian Williams	Rugby (NZ)
Michael Dods	Rugby (Scotland)
Shane Warne	Cricket
Alec Stewart	Cricket
Graham Thorpe	Cricket
Chris Cairns	Cricket
Chris Cowdrey	Cricket
David Smith	Cricket
Johnny Herbert	Motor Racing
Daley Thompson	Decathlete
Joe Calzaghe	Boxing
Boris Becker	Tennis
Pat Cash	Tennis
Peter Fleming	Tennis
Dick Francis	Horse Racing

ABOVE A Major Chelsea fan

BELOW Lord Sebastian Coe

BELOW LEFT Jimmy White, Chelsea fan

FAMOUS FANS

RIGHT Boris Becker

BELOW Johnny Vaughan

William Jarvis	Horse Racing
Mark Winstanley	Horse Racing
Mark Hughes	Football
Paul McGrath	Football
Paul Merson	Football
Mark Wright	Football

TV & Film

Johnny Vaughan	Presenter
Andy Jacobs	Presenter Talksport
Tim Lovejoy	Presenter
David Baddiel	Comedian
Clare Balding	TV & Radio broadcaster
Sir Jeremy Isaacs	Producer/Director
Chris Barrie	Actor/Comedian (Red Dwarf)
Lord Attenborough (former Life President)	Film Director (Died 2014)
Sir John Mills	Actor (Died 2005)
Sir Laurence Olivier	Actor (Died 2005)
Michael Crawford	Actor
Russell Grant	Astrologer
Richard O'Sullivan	Actor
Rodney Bewes	Actor (Likely Lads)
Bill Oddie	Comedian/ TV Presenter
Gabriel Byrne	Actor
Joseph Fiennes	Actor

Dennis Waterman	Actor
Phil Daniels	Actor
Dorian Healy	Actor
Michael Greco	Actor
Michael Caine	Actor
Bruce Dern	Actor
Raquel Welch	Actress
Derek Fowlds	Actor (Heartbeat)
Bill Nighy	Actor
Dervla Kirwan	Actress, (Ballykissangel)
Trevor Eve	Actor
David Redfearn	Magician
Graham King	Movie Producer
Tom Pollock	Film director
Sean Lock	Comedian
Huw Higginson	Actor
Henry Kelly	Game Show Host
Jason Fleming	Actor (Snatch)
Guy Ritchie	Director

Music

Bryan Adams	Musician
Suggs (Lead Singer with Madness)	(Singer)
Daniel Woodgate (Woody)	Drummer (Madness)
Paul Hardcastle	Recording Artist (19)
Joe Strummer (Ex The Clash)	Musician (Died 2002)
Paul Cook	Musician (Sex Pistols)
Steve Jones	Musician (Sex Pistols)
Morten Harket	Singer (A-Ha)
Jimmy Page	Musician (Led Zeppelin)
John Taylor	Musician (Duran Duran)
Alan McGee	Head of Creation Records (Oasis)
Andy Fletcher	Musician (Depeche Mode)
Dave Gahan	Singer (Depeche Mode)
Lloyd Cole	Musician
Nik Kershaw	80's Pop star
Busta Rhymes	US Rap star
Gary Numan	80's Pop star
Andy Cairns	Lead Singer (Therapy)
Ed Ball	Musician
Charlie Harper	Musician (UK Subs)
Alex Paterson	Musician (The Orb)
John O'Neill	Musician (The Undertones)
Paul Oakenfold	DJ/Producer
Trevor Nelson	DJ (Radio 1)
Graham Dene	DJ
Jeff Young	DJ
Paul Anderson	DJ (Xfm)
Tim Simenon	DJ, Producer (Depeche Mode)
Gary Crowley	DJ
Gilles Peterson	DJ
Iain Baker	DJ (Xfm), Musician (Jesus Jones)
Damon Albarn	Lead Singer (Blur & Gorillaz)
Seb Fontaine	DJ (Radio 1)
Ian Collins	Radio presenter (Talksport)
Geri Halliwell	Singer

Writers/Journalists

Roddy Doyle	Playwright
Andy Hamilton	Comedy Writer
Jeremy Vine	News presenter
Mark Austin	News Presenter (Sky)
Giles Smith	News Presenter (Sky)

BELOW Guy Ritchie

ABOVE Michael Caine

BELOW LEFT Ex-Spice Girl Geri Halliwell

BELOW RIGHT Blur's Damon Albarn

Nigel Clarke	Football Writer (Mirror)
John Motson	Commentator (can't admit it)
Martin Tyler	Commentator (a soft spot at least)
John Moynihan	Journalist/Author
Shelly Webb	TV Presenter and wife of former player Neil Webb
Albert Sewell	Match of the Day stats man (died 2013)
Adam Porter	Journalist (Loaded magazine)

Miscellaneous

Vidal Sassoon	Hairdresser
Toni Frei	Travel
Mick Taylor	British Airways
Russell Terrett	Anglo Nordic Burner
Ollie Gammond	Sky Media
Perry Keena	Financial Management
Stephen Kelly	Business mentor
Martine Pugh	Publishing
Stephen Bendall	Banking (retired)
Martin Greenslade	Police (retired)
Tim Barnes	Leasing (retired)

Ferreira

ABOVE Paulo Ferreira stretches to reach the ball first

Never flashy but always dependable, Paulo Ferreira was a reliable presence in the Chelsea team for more than 200 appearances over a ten-year period.

After playing for Porto for two years (where he won the Champions League Final), Paulo Ferreira joined Chelsea for £13.2 million at the beginning of the 2004-05 season reuniting him with his former manager Jose Mourinho and team-mate Ricardo Carvalho.

Ferreira impressed greatly in his debut season, playing 29 Premier League matches before injury ruled him out for the remainder of the campaign. He continued his fine form into the following campaign, during which he scored his first Chelsea goal in the 3-1 victory over Colchester United in the FA Cup fourth round.

Despite becoming a regular on his manager's team sheet, Ferreira suffered from a lack of confidence in the 2006-07 season, which eventually saw him lose his place to first Boulahrouz and then to midfielder Geremi. However he did play the full 120 minutes of Chelsea's 1-0 FA Cup Final win over Manchester United.

Ferreira was the second choice right-back for Chelsea during the 2007-08 season behind Michael Essien and Juliano Belletti. When played, Ferreira was his usual consistent self, putting in unspectacular, workman like performances. As Mourinho so aptly put it "Paulo is a player who will never be Man of the Match but will always score 7/10 for his individual display."

Very quietly, he won three Premier League titles, four FA Cups, two Football League Cups and received a winners medal as an unused substitute in the Champions League Final against Bayern Munich in 2012 in Munich as he had featured in previous fixtures in the run up to the final.

He played his last match for Chelsea in a 2-1 win over Everton in May 2013 and at the end of the match, thought that was as good as time as any to hang up his boots. But he is now back at the Bridge as part of Frank Lampard's coaching team.

Flo

RIGHT Tore Andre Flo being welcomed back onto the Stamford Bridge pitch in 2018

When it comes to returns on investment there can be few as profitable as Tore Andre Flo, who arrived at Chelsea in the summer of 1997 as a £300,000 signing from Brann Bergen in his native Norway.

Three seasons later, with 50 first team goals to his name, he departed in a £12 million deal to Rangers and a reputation as a predatory finisher if not the most elegant of players.

Tore scored as a sub on his Chelsea debut, a 2-1 defeat to Coventry, and went on to regularly make an impact from the bench as he helped the team to FA Cup, League Cup and UEFA Cup Winners' Cup successes, as well as bagging a hat-trick at White Hart Lane in a 6-1 victory over Spurs in late 1997 - that achievement alone earning him lasting affection with fans.

The lanky striker also helped Chelsea to qualify for the Champions League for the first time in 1999, and scored eight times in that campaign, including three against Barcelona as the team controversially bowed out in the quarter-finals.

Hugely popular at Stamford Bridge, Flo is one of four ex-players to be an ambassador at the club and regularly attends games reminding guests of his famous hat-trick against Spurs!

Guus

ABOVE Guus Hiddink lifts the trophy after the FA Cup Final between Chelsea and Everton, 2009

After the sacking of former Brazilian manager Luiz Felipe Scolari half-way through the 2008-09 season, Chelsea appointed the Guus Hiddink as his replacement until the end of the season.

He had previously won the European Cup with PSV and in the same tournament won his first game in charge at Stamford Bridge with a 1-0 victory over Juventus. Success continued in the form of a 3-1 away victory against Liverpool – commentators stating that Guus had rejuvenated Chelsea following Scolari's departure.

After knocking Liverpool out of the competition, Guus went on to take Chelsea to the semi-finals of the Champions League where they unluckily lost out to eventual winners Barcelona in the 93rd minute after a 1-1 draw at Stamford Bridge.

Guus only lost once during his tenure as Chelsea manager, a 1-0 defeat at White Hart Lane where Luka Modric scored the only goal of the match. In the final home game of the season, in which Chelsea beat Blackburn Rovers 2-0, fans chanted his name throughout the match and called for Chelsea owner Roman Abramovich to "sign him up" (on a permanent basis).

Guus's highly positive reception highlighted the Chelsea fans' appreciation of the manager. In his last game as a temporary coach of Chelsea, he won the 2009 FA Cup by beating Everton 2-1 at Wembley.

Nearly six years after this departure, he was again appointed interim manager in December 2015 until the end of the season following the sacking of Jose Mourinho; and in that time set a record for a run of 12 undefeated matches by a new Premiership manager. In the twilight of a long and distinguished playing and managerial career, he now coaches the Chinese under-21s team.

Greatest XI

To celebrate Chelsea's centenary, the fans selected their Greatest Ever XI via a poll on the club's website. The winners were …

Manager
Jose Mourinho

1	Peter Bonetti
2	Steve Clarke
3	John Terry
4	Marcel Desailly
5	Graham Le Saux
6	Frank Lampard
7	Dennis Wise
8	Charlie Cooke
9	Gianfranco Zola
10	Peter Osgood
11	Bobby Tambling

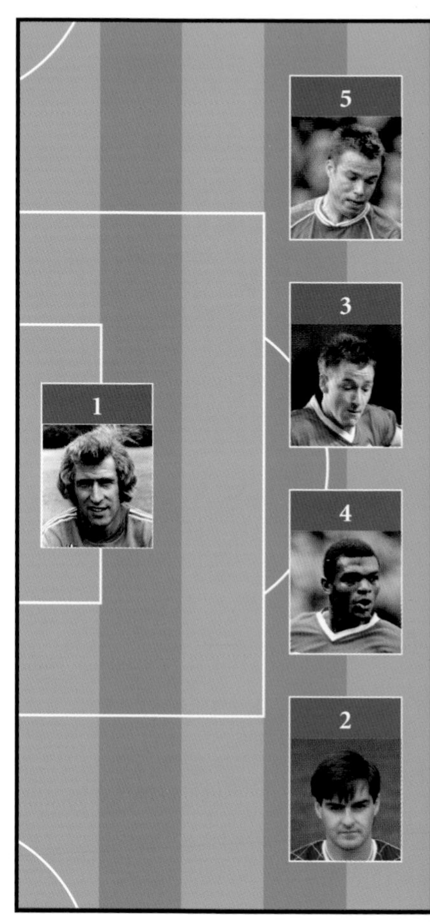

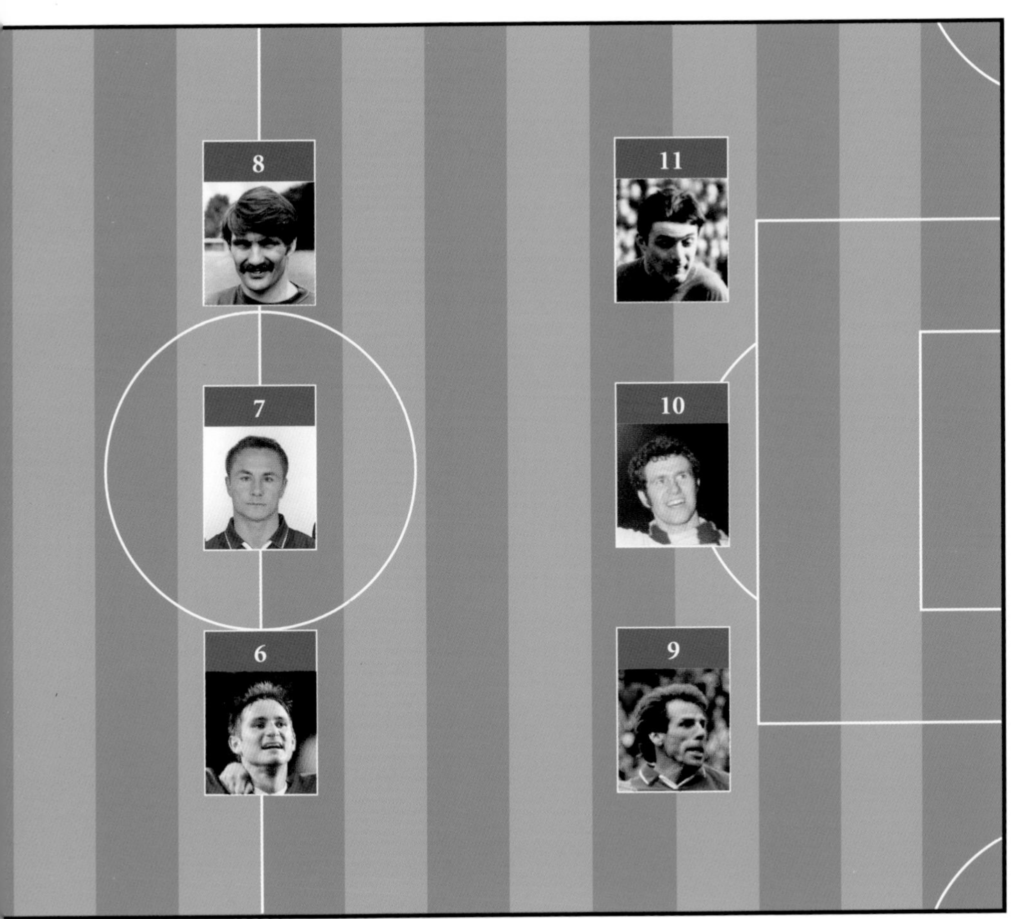
8
11
7
10
6
9

Greaves

RIGHT AND OPPOSITE Jimmy Greaves in training at Stamford Bridge

Jimmy Greaves was a prolific goalscorer wherever he played but it is not readily remembered that he made a name for himself at Chelsea before becoming a Spurs' legend.

Courted by many clubs in his youth and widely expected to join Spurs, Greaves signed with Chelsea as a junior in 1955 and made his debut for the first team two years later, scoring Chelsea's goal in the 1-1 draw.

By the 1958-59 season he was a regular in the team, netting 32 goals to finish the top goalscorer in the First Division (the first of six occasions Jimmy headed the goalscoring list) and going on to make his England debut (he scored England's goal in the 4-1 defeat by Peru).

In 1960-61 he again topped the goalscoring charts, netting 41 goals and establishing Chelsea's highest number of goals in a season. By then there were rumblings that Greaves might be on his way out of the club, for with players still subject to the maximum wage of £20, a few were tempted by moves to Italy

where wages were considerably higher. He signed a deal with AC Milan that was worth £80,000 to Chelsea, although by the time the deal went through the maximum wage had been lifted and Chelsea and the player unsuccessfully attempted to get the deal cancelled. Never able to settle in Italy, despite scoring on his debut, by December 1961 Chelsea and Spurs were bidding to get him back into English football. Chelsea would not go above the £80,000 they had received for him, leaving Spurs to clinch his signature for a figure that was reported to be £99,999, or £1 off £100,000 as Spurs' manager Bill Nicholson didn't want him saddled with the tag of being the first player to have cost such a sum.

He needn't have worried, for inside the penalty area nothing phased Greaves, as his League record of 357 goals in 514 games and 44 goals for England in 57 appearances would confirm. In March 1970 he moved on to West Ham United where he retired in 1971. He battled with alcoholism for much of his life but became an entertaining television pundit forming a hilarious double act with Ian St. John. In May 2015 he suffered a massive stroke and is now on the slow road to recovery.

Gudjohnsen

Although the nomadic Icelandic footballer Eidur Gudjohnsen has played for myriad clubs across Europe, he is still held in great affection by Chelsea fans following his six seasons at the club.

He was signed in the summer of 2000 from Bolton Wanderers for a fee of £4 million by Gianluca Vialli and formed a deadly partnership with Dutch striker Jimmy Floyd Hasselbaink during the 2001-02 season scoring 23 goals himself and helping Hasselbaink to a tally of 27.

His dribbling and close-control, combined with his sublime finishing, saw him score some remarkable goals during his time at Chelsea the best of which was probably his overhead kick against Leeds in the 2002-03 season.

While big name strikers came and went at the club his deft touches and vision saw him used in a more supportive attacking role behind the front men although he still scored more than 70 goals in 261 appearances.

His unique claim to fame occurred in April 1996 when he and his father created football history during the Icelandic friendly international against

OPPOSITE Eidur Gudjohnsen in action against Aston Villa

LEFT Eidur Gudjohnsen celebrates winning the 2004-5 Premier League with Frank Lampard and John Terry

Estonia. During the second half Eidur replaced his father Arnor, the first time a father and son had played in the same international match.

Gullit

RIGHT Ruud Gullit
BELOW Player/ Manager Gullit in control

Ruud Gullit may have been past his sell-by date when he signed for Chelsea in 1995, yet the former World Player of the Year showed that class is permanent in a deeper play-making midfield position. As player-manager, he also guided the club to an FA Cup Final victory in 1997.

Born in Amsterdam on 1 September 1962, he was brought up in Amsterdam and signed for the local DWS Amsterdam as a schoolboy. He then switched to Haarlem and developed into an exciting midfield prospect, subsequently be-ing snapped up by Feyenoord in 1982 where he played alongside Johan Cruyff and helped them to the double of League and cup in 1984

In 1985 he moved on to PSV Eindhoven, helping them win the Dutch League in consecutive seasons (1986 and 1987). A £6 million transfer took him to AC Milan in 1987, linking up with fellow countrymen Marco Van Basten and Frank Rijkaard, winning three Serie A titles and the European Cup twice.

In 1993 he moved on to Sampdoria, where he won the Italian Cup, returned briefly to AC Milan and brought to a close his Italian venture with a second stint at Sampdoria.

In 1995 he was one of the key players brought in to Chelsea by Glenn Hoddle and, although not the same as far as pace was concerned, his tactical awareness and ability on the ball made him a star performer. When Hoddle left to take on the England manager's job

Ruud was appointed player-manager, subsequently guiding the club to FA Cup victory in 1997.

Despite this success Ruud was sacked in February 1998 and subsequently re-surfaced at Newcastle United. He resigned after five games of the 2000-01 season and had a spell out of the game before becoming coach at Feyenoord in 2004 and resigning again at the end of the season. He is now a television pundit.

A former European Footballer of the Year (in 1987) and World Player of the Year in 1987 and 1989, he helped Holland to their only major tournament triumph, the European Championship in 1988.

ABOVE Chelsea Manager Ruud Gullit holds the FA Cup after the win against Middlesbourgh

Harding

A life-long supporter of Chelsea, Matthew Harding became more closely involved in the club after answering a call for investors from Ken Bates.

Born on 26 December 1953, Matthew left school with one A level and worked at a couple of banks before landing a job with a new re-insurance company Benfields.

He started as a junior in 1973 and acquired a part of the company in 1980, subsequently acquiring a sizeable share two years later. By the 1990s his share was worth over £150 million and he was a member of the most exclusive of all clubs, the Top 100 Rich List.

In 1994 he agreed to invest some of his sizeable fortune in Chelsea, having been a regular at Stamford Bridge since the age of eight. His investment of some £26.5 million, including £5 million that was spent on the new North Stand, earned him a position of vice-chairman alongside Ken Bates, but the two men were soon involved in a feud, disagreeing over matters such as how the ground should be developed.

Ken Bates, often confrontational, took to banning Matthew Harding from the directors box at Stamford Bridge, with Matthew going off to sit in the North Stand.

Although the pair eventually agreed on a truce, it was always uneasy, but nothing could prevent Matthew from

following his beloved Chelsea.

On 22 October 1996, whilst returning home from a night match at Bolton, the helicopter in which he was a passenger crashed, killing all the occupants. Before his death he had said that his dream was to see players of the calibre of Charlie Cooke and Peter Osgood, winning the FA Cup and Cup Winners Cup in successive seasons back at Stamford Bridge. Two years after his death Chelsea did just that.

ABOVE Matthew Harding applauds fans from his seat in the North Stand

LEFT A tribute in memory of Matthew Harding

ABOVE Chopper and his 1970 troops

RIGHT Chelsea captain Ron Harris holds aloft the European Cup Winners' Cup after beating Real Madrid 2-1 in a replay

OPPOSITE Stamford Bridge - the garden of Eden

Harris

Ron 'Chopper' Harris was the epitome of loyalty to the Chelsea cause.

Born in Hackney on 13 November 1944, he joined Chelsea as a junior in 1960, following his brother Allan, and signed professional forms in November 1961. Over the next 19 years Ron amassed a total of 795 appearances for the club, still the record, and he has deservedly had a suite names after him at the Bridge.

He was appointed captain when Terry Venables moved on and led the club to glory in the FA Cup in 1970 and the European Cup Winners Cup the following year when beating the mighty Real Madrid.

Capped four times at Under 23 level, Ron was unfortunate never to have earned a full cap for his country, especially at a time when England needed a midfield destroyer, a role Ron Harris excelled at.

Known affectionately as Chopper on account of the ferocity of his tackles, Ron left Chelsea in May 1980 and wound down his career at Brentford, finally retiring from playing in 1983. He later toured the after dinner speaker circuit, often in company with former Chelsea player Jimmy Greaves. and is still a regular at the Bridge in an ambassadorial role.

Hasselbaink

Jimmy Floyd Hasselbaink played for ten clubs over 18 seasons, scoring 245 goals in the process, but it is as a Chelsea player that his career is best remembered.

Jimmy was a club record signing when he joined form Atletico Madrid in 2000. The fee of £15m could be considered a bargain as he averaged nearly a goal every two games over the next four years.

He scored in his first game for the club, the Charity Shield against Manchester United and finished the year with 26 goals. The following year he formed a prolific telepathic partnership with Eidur Gudjohnsen and together their goals helped Chelsea reach the FA Cup Final. Unfortunately, Jimmy was injured in the league game prior to the final and was clearly unfit before eventually being substituted.

Although the goals somewhat dried up over the next two years, he helped Chelsea to qualify for the Champions League on both occasions. In March 2004 he scored a hat-trick in a win over Wolverhampton Wanderers becoming the only player in Chelsea's history to score three times after coming off of the bench.

Jimmy left in the summer of 2004 as the new manager looked to bring in his own players. He joined Middlesbrough and later played for Charlton and Cardiff. Ironically, he scored his first Charlton goal at Stamford Bridge and he earned an ovation from the home fans as he refused to celebrate.

BELOW Jimmy Floyd Hasselbaink celebrates scoring another goal in a Chelsea shirt

Hazard

Very few Chelsea fans blamed Eden Hazard for leaving the club to go to his dream team Real Madrid in the summer of 2019 after all the entertainment and trophies he provided during his seven years at the Bridge.

He helped the team win two Premier Leagues, two Europa Leagues and the FA Cup and the League Cup; and was voted Chelsea Player of the Year a record four times. In all he played 352 games for the club and scored 110 goals – putting him in the Top Ten goal-scorers in the history of the club.

BELOW Eden Hazard celebrates winning the Europa League final against Arsenal in his last match for Chelsea

He was a truly word-class player – probably just a notch below Messi and Ronaldo but at that level – with a low centre of gravity and lightning turn of pace, who could leave defenders for dead. Fans would automatically stand up when he had the ball at his feet, never sure what would happen.

Hazard signed for Chelsea for £32 million in June 2012 and while the club made around £100 million profit when selling him to Real Madrid in June 2019, everyone wished he had stayed as he was still only 28.

He signed off with a fairy-tale finish scoring two goals, and providing an assist for Pedro, in Chelsea's 4-1 thrashing of Arsenal in the Europa Cup Final in May 2019. Alongside Zola, he was the best player ever to wear the Blue of Chelsea and his legacy will not be forgotten.

As Chelsea director Marina Granoyskaia commented: "The memories he leaves with us will not fade. He provided all who watched Chelsea play with great entertainment and many match-winning contributions. "

Hollins

John Hollins gave Chelsea exceptional service over a quarter of a century, twice in spells as a player and once as manager.

Born in Guildford on 16 July 1946 into a footballing family (his father played for Stoke and Wolves whilst his brother was with Newcastle and Mansfield) he signed professional forms with Chelsea in July 1963 and quickly established himself as the human dynamo of the side with his non-stop running.

John's first spell at Stamford Bridge was to last until June 1975 when he was transferred to Queen's Park Rangers, after 436 League appearances for the club (he scored 47 goals).

John remained at Loftus Road for four years before moving to North London and signing for Arsenal, supposedly in the twilight of his career, but he went on to top the hundred mark for League appearances for the third time (he made 151 appearances for QPR) over the next three years, racking up 127 appearances for the Gunners. Even then John's career was not at an end, for in June 1983, at the age of 37, he returned to Stamford Bridge a second time to finish out his playing days.

After 29 turnouts John finally called it a day and moved into coaching. When John Neal was moved from manager to director in 1985, John stepped into the manager's role and served in that capacity for three years.

BELOW John Hollins about to cross the ball into the box

ABOVE John Hollins (left) in action

ABOVE RIGHT John Hollins

Had John not left Stamford Bridge in 1975 it is quite conceivable that he would have registered the club's greatest tally of appearances.

Although he won numerous caps at youth, Under 23 and B level, John was unfortunate to have been picked for the full England side on only one occasion, but in so doing he created something of a record that may never be beaten; his brother had previously been capped for Wales!

Hudson

Born just around the corner from Stamford Bridge, Alan Hudson signed schoolboy forms with Chelsea before being taken on as an apprentice in 1966.

Upgraded to the professional ranks in June 1968, he quickly established a reputation as an exciting, flair player and was seemingly on his way to writing a large part in the Chelsea history book for himself.

Troubled by injuries throughout his career, he was forced to sit out as Chelsea won the FA Cup in 1970 but was an integral part of the side that lifted the European Cup Winners' Cup the following season.

His undoubted abilities on the pitch were frequently rocked by revelations and upsets off it and in January 1974 the golden boy of Chelsea was sold to Stoke City for £240,000. His arrival coincided in an upturn in fortunes for the Potteries club, but in December 1976, having fallen out with the manager and with the club in desperate need of money, he was sold back to London, this time to Arsenal, for £180,000.

A runners-up medal in the 1978 FA Cup was the highlight of his brief stay at Highbury and in October 1978 he was on his way again, heading over the Atlantic to join Seattle Sounders for £100,000.

He was to enjoy the less intense

BELOW Alan Hudson chased by another London legend Stan Bowles

ABOVE LEFT Huddy the Hunk

ABOVE RIGHT Alan Hudson celebrates with team-mates after their victory over Real Madrid in the European Cup Winners' Cup Final in Athens

atmosphere of North American football for almost five years before returning to Stamford Bridge in August 1983, but failed to make the first team and moved back to Stoke City.

As club captain Hudson made 39 appearances for Stoke during his second spell with the club, finally calling time on his career owing to injury at the age of 34. Whilst fans of Chelsea, Stoke and Arsenal will argue long and hard as to who had the best out of Hudson during his club career, there is no doubt he was sadly wasted at international level, collecting only two caps.

His abilities with the ball were unquestioned, but perhaps, like Stan Bowles, Frank Worthington and Tony Currie, doubts about other aspects of his game and lifestyle counted against him when it came to selecting the England side.

Hutchinson

Ian Hutchinson's was a career that promised much but fell short of expectations in the final analysis.

Born in Derby on 4 August 1975, he spent a season with Nottingham Forest as an amateur before joining Cambridge United, then a non-League side and was spotted by Chelsea in 1968. He moved to Stamford Bridge in July 1968 and quickly established himself in the first team, but his all-action style frequently saw him sidelined by injuries, some serious, such as a broken leg and nose, others more minor.

He did play an important part in the FA Cup win in 1970, scoring in the first, drawn match with a header (he even out-jumped Jack Charlton!) and firing in one of his speciality long throws from which David Webb scored the winner in the replay.

That was to be the peak of his Chelsea career unfortunately, for continued struggles to overcome a succession of injuries saw him make just 119 League appearances for the Blues before he retired in 1975. Ian died on September 19, 2002 after a lengthy illness.

BELOW Ian Hutchinson

RIGHT Hutchinson launches one of his long throws

Ivanovic

Football runs in Branislav Ivanovic's family – he is related to the late Dorde Milanovic and his son Dejan, both of whom are well known to Red Star Belgrade fans, and his father was also a pro. Perhaps it was inevitable that he should end up making his living from the beautiful game, but it was far from pre-ordained that he should be making that living in West London.

Born in Sremska Mitrovica, Serbia on 22 February 1984, the tall young defender first turned out for his father's old club, Srem, before moving on to OFK Beograd and then making his first move to a foreign club, Lokomotiv Moscow, in 2006. There he made 54 appearances, weighing in with five goals, while also making a name for himself in the Serbian national side.

A 2007 Russian Cup winner's medal was the only addition to his mantelpiece during his stay in Moscow, and Branislav was clearly seeking more silverware when he was transferred to Chelsea in January 2008 for a fee reported to be £9.7 million – the biggest in Russian football history according to Lokomotiv.

Large fee notwithstanding, it took a while for the Serbian to establish himself but he truly announced his arrival on the scene with a legendary brace at Anfield in a Champions League quarter-final tie against regular European foes Liverpool.

The following 2009/10 campaign, Ivanovic's discipline, tough tackling and marauding forward runs from right-back earned him a place in the PFA Team of the Year and he was winning over the Blues' faithful.

His versatility meant he was equally adept in the centre of defence as on the right, and he performed with remarkable

LEFT Branislav Ivanovic in action

consistency in both positions. He was always highly valued by managers, team-mates and supporters alike, who recognised his exceptional commitment to the Chelsea cause, as well as his happy knack of finding the net.

It was Ivanovic who popped up with the amazing winning goal against Napoli when the team's run to Champions League glory in 2012 caught fire, and it was Ivanovic who headed the glorious injury-time winner in the Europa League final the following year. Ivanovic was outstanding during the title-winning 2014/15 campaign and played all but a few minutes of all 38 games, again named in the Team of the Year.

He captained the team towards the end of his Chelsea career, testament to his leadership qualities and love for the club. In total he made 377 appearances during his nine years in West London, scoring 34 times.

Kante

For a little man N'Golo Kante was a big addition to the squad for the 2016/17 season as he was at that time the best defensive midfielder in the world.

Kante joined from Leicester City where he so memorably played a major part in the Foxes' miraculous Premier League triumph against all the odds. The then 25-year-old came close to adding to that success on the international stage as France was denied a host-team triumph at Euro 2016 by an extra-time Portugal goal in the final.

Picking up where he had left off at Leicester, Kante was a mainstay of Antonio Conte's team in the first half of the campaign, memorably scoring the fourth and final goal in a big win over Manchester United in October 2016.

His tireless efficiency as a covering midfielder earned him the PFA Player of the Year award and the Footballer of the Year by the Football Writers' Association, becoming one of only a few players to win both awards in the same season.

Most importantly, he started 35 of the 38 games that recaptured the Premier League title for Chelsea becoming the first player to win successive Premier League titles with two different clubs.

Kante's performances in the following season remained at a high level even when the team struggled around him. He was a star man in both legs of the Champions League last 16 tie against Barcelona, especially impressing in Camp Nou, and played a key role as Chelsea reached the FA Cup final.

Before the Wembley showpiece, Kante's performances during 2017/18 season were recognised by the Chelsea supporters who voted him their Player of the Year. He then ended the season on a high, shining in midfield yet again as the Blues shut out Man United to secure the FA Cup, the first of Kante's career.

Kante began life under Maurizio Sarri in a new unfamiliar role, slightly further forward on the right of a three-man midfield, but he was never as effective – and the manager's stubbornness created a wedge between Sarri and the fans. Why play the best defensive midfield player in the world out of position!?

Although not looking comfortable in his new role, he was typically consistent as Chelsea secured a top-four position, but a hamstring injury sustained against Watford in the penultimate league game meant his place in the Europa League final starting XI was in serious jeopardy. Happily, he battled through to start in Baku and help us to a big win over Arsenal.

His crowning glory as an international player came in 2018 when he was part of the French team that beat Croatia 4-2 in the final of the World Cup in Paris adding to his burgeoning medal collection.

BELOW N'Golo Kante putting in another tireless performance

Lampard

ABOVE Super Frank!

That Frank Lampard was worshipped as a Chelsea player was unquestioned – whether he will be seen as a 'super' manager remains to be seen.

The fans will give him time, as one of their own, and because of his legendary status as the club's all-time record goal scorer with 211 goals in 648 games, placing him as the fourth highest player in terms of appearances behind Ron Harris, Peter Bonetti and his captain John Terry.

His appointment as manager in July 2019 was a risk after he had led Derby County to the play-off finals in his first season as a boss but he was seen as a welcome alternative to the succession of moody mercenary Continental managers whose love affair with the club was largely based on the level of their pay.

The gamble seemed to pay off in the early part of his first season as, after losing 4-0 to Manchester United in the opening match, his young players (which he blooded in the first team because of a transfer ban) propelled him into the top four and he won Premier League Manager of the Month for October.

Lampard loves Chelsea and even if he is sacked as manager, it shouldn't diminish his standing as one of the greatest players in the club's, and Premier League's history.

Once hailed by Mourinho as the best player in the world, his greatest assets were his long-range shooting and the ability to drift into the box unnoticed.

He began his career at West Ham United where his father, Frank Senior, was a former player and assistant manager, while his uncle, Harry Redknapp, was manager.He helped the team to their highest-ever Premier League finishing position in the 1998-99 season and the following season he scored 14 goals in all competitions from midfield. With progress stagnating at West Ham, he moved to rivals Chelsea in 2001 for £11 million.

From his debut onwards he was ever-present in the Chelsea first team, setting a record 164 consecutive Premier League appearances. Under new manager

ABOVE Frank relaxes with author Jules Gammond on the eve of the Champions' League Final in Moscow

ABOVE RIGHT Master and Commander

RIGHT It was inevitable that Super Frank would score when playing for Man City against Chelsea in 2015

Mourinho he won his first major honours in 2005, winning the Premier League and League Cup and again won the League and a domestic Cup Double in 2007. By the end of his Chelsea career he had amassed three Premier League titles, four FA Cups, two Football League Cups, the Europa League title and the Champions League trophy in 2012.

Internationally, he became one of a select band of players to play more than one hundred times for his country, scoring some 29 goals from midfield placing him in the English Top Ten Scorers of all time.

He reluctantly left Chelsea at the end of the 2014 season to play in America for New York City who are owned by Manchester City. The Manchester club needing cover in their midfield loaned him back for the season and he subsequently played some 38 games for them scoring eight goals. He came on as a substitute for City to play against Chelsea and typically scored their only goal in a 1-1 draw – refusing to celebrate out of respect to the club he continues to serve so long and so well.

League Positions

Season Ending	Division	Position	P	W	D	L	F	A	Points
1906	2	3rd	38	22	9	7	90	37	53
1907	2	2nd	38	26	5	7	80	34	57
1908	1	13th	38	14	8	16	53	62	36
1909	1	11th	38	14	9	15	56	61	37
1910	1	19th	38	11	7	20	47	70	29
1911	2	3rd	38	20	9	9	71	35	49
1912	2	2nd	38	24	6	8	74	34	54
1913	1	18th	38	11	6	21	51	73	28
1914	1	8th	38	16	7	15	46	55	39
1915	1	19th	38	8	13	17	51	65	29
1920	1	3rd	42	22	5	15	56	51	49
1921	1	18th	42	13	13	16	48	58	39
1922	1	9th	42	17	12	13	40	43	46
1923	1	19th	42	9	18	15	45	53	36
1924	1	21st	42	9	14	19	31	53	32
1925	2	5th	42	16	15	11	51	37	47
1926	2	3rd	42	19	14	9	76	49	52
1927	2	4th	42	20	12	10	62	52	52
1928	2	3rd	42	23	8	11	75	45	54
1929	2	9th	42	17	10	15	64	65	44
1930	2	2nd	42	22	11	9	74	46	55
1931	1	12th	42	15	10	17	64	67	40
1932	1	12th	42	16	8	18	69	73	40
1933	1	12th	42	14	7	21	63	73	35
1934	1	19th	42	14	8	20	67	69	36
1935	1	12th	42	16	9	17	73	82	41
1936	1	8th	42	15	13	14	65	72	43
1937	1	13th	42	14	13	15	52	55	41
1938	1	10th	42	14	13	15	65	65	41
1939	1	20th	42	12	9	21	64	80	33
1940	1	12th	3	1	1	1	4	4	3

ABOVE Chelsea flag

LEAGUE POSITIONS

Season Ending	Division	Position	P	W	D	L	F	A	Points
1947	1	15th	42	16	7	19	69	84	39
1948	1	18th	42	14	9	19	53	71	37
1949	1	13th	42	12	14	16	69	68	38
1950	1	13th	42	12	16	14	58	65	40
1951	1	20th	42	12	8	22	53	65	32
1952	1	19th	42	14	8	20	52	72	36
1953	1	19th	42	12	11	19	56	66	35
1954	1	8th	42	16	12	14	74	68	44
1955	1	1st	42	20	12	10	81	57	52
1956	1	16th	42	14	11	17	64	77	39
1957	1	13th	42	13	13	16	73	73	39
1958	1	11th	42	15	12	15	83	79	42
1959	1	14th	42	18	4	20	77	98	40
1960	1	18th	42	14	9	19	76	91	37
1961	1	12th	42	15	7	20	98	100	37
1962	1	22nd	42	9	10	23	63	94	28
1963	2	2nd	42	24	4	14	81	42	52
1964	1	5th	42	20	10	12	72	56	50
1965	1	3rd	42	24	8	10	89	54	56
1966	1	5th	42	22	7	13	65	53	51
1967	1	9th	42	15	14	13	67	62	44
1968	1	6th	42	18	12	12	62	68	48
1969	1	5th	42	20	10	12	73	53	50
1970	1	3rd	42	21	13	8	70	50	55
1971	1	6th	42	18	15	9	52	42	51
1972	1	7th	42	18	12	12	58	49	48
1973	1	12th	42	13	14	15	49	51	40
1974	1	17th	42	12	13	17	56	60	37
1975	1	21st	42	9	15	18	42	72	33
1976	2	11th	42	12	16	14	53	54	40
1977	2	2nd	42	21	13	8	73	53	55
1978	1	16th	42	11	14	17	46	69	36
1979	1	22nd	42	5	10	27	44	92	20
1980	2	4th	42	23	7	12	66	52	53
1981	2	12th	42	14	12	16	46	41	40

BELOW Young Chelsea supporters

LEAGUE POSITIONS

Season Ending	Division	Position	P	W	D	L	F	A	Points
1982	2	12th	42	15	12	15	60	60	57
1983	2	18th	42	11	14	17	51	61	47
1984	2	1st	42	25	13	4	80	40	88
1985	1	6th	42	18	12	12	63	48	66
1986	1	6th	42	20	11	11	57	56	71
1987	1	14th	42	13	13	16	53	64	52
1988	1	18th	40	9	15	16	50	68	42
1989	2	1st	46	29	12	5	96	50	99
1990	1	5th	38	16	12	10	58	50	60
1991	1	11th	38	13	10	15	58	69	49
1992	1	14th	42	13	14	15	50	60	53
1993	Prem	11th	42	14	14	14	51	54	56
1994	Prem	14th	42	13	12	17	49	53	51
1995	Prem	11th	42	13	15	14	50	55	54
1996	Prem	11th	38	12	14	12	46	44	50
1997	Prem	6th	38	16	11	11	58	55	59
1998	Prem	4th	38	20	3	15	71	43	63
1999	Prem	3rd	38	20	15	3	57	30	75
2000	Prem	5th	38	18	11	9	53	34	65
2001	Prem	6th	38	17	10	11	68	45	61
2002	Prem	6th	38	17	13	8	66	38	64
2003	Prem	4th	38	19	10	9	67	38	67
2004	Prem	2nd	38	24	7	7	67	30	79
2005	Prem	1st	38	29	8	1	72	15	95
2006	Prem	1st	38	29	4	5	72	22	91
2007	Prem	2nd	38	34	11	3	64	24	83
2008	Prem	2nd	38	25	10	3	65	26	85
2009	Prem	3rd	38	25	8	5	68	24	83
2010	Prem	1st	38	27	5	6	103	32	86
2011	Prem	2nd	38	21	8	9	69	33	71
2012	Prem	6th	38	18	10	10	65	46	64
2013	Prem	3rd	38	22	9	7	75	39	75
2014	Prem	3rd	38	25	7	6	71	27	82
2015	Prem	1st	38	26	9	3	73	32	87
2016	Prem	10th	38	12	14	12	59	53	50
2017	Prem	1st	38	30	3	5	85	33	93
2018	Prem	5th	38	21	7	10	62	38	70
2019	Prem	3rd	38	21	9	8	63	39	72

ABOVE Exterior of Stamford Bridge

BELOW The always stylish Frank Leboeuf

Leboeuf

A stylish French defender, Frank Leboeuf was one of the first wave of foreigners to light up the Premier League in the mid-1990s.

Intelligent and composed, Leboeuf won both the World Cup and European Championship while a Chelsea player, and was a regular scorer of penalties and long-range goals during his time with the club which lasted 204 games over five years.

Leboeuf arrived from Strasbourg in the summer of 1996 and would go on to forge an effective complimentary partnership with his French patriot Marcel Desailly in the centre of defence during one of Chelsea's most successful periods.

His Chelsea CV boasts The FA Cup in 1997, followed by the League Cup, the UEFA Cup Winners Cup and the UEFA Super Cup a year later, all won with clean sheets, as was the FA Cup again in 2000, the last final at the old Wembley.

Leboeuf returned to France with Marseille in 2001 before finishing his career in Qatar. He has since pursued a career in the film industry.

Le Saux

Born on the island of Jersey , Graeme Le Saux began his career at Chelsea in 1987 and spent six seasons at Stamford Bridge during his first spell with the club, making 110 League appearances.

The closest he came to establishing himself as a first team regular came during the 1991-92 season when he made 40 League appearances, but in 1993 he moved to Blackburn Rovers.

A member of the side that finished runners up and then Champions in the Premiership in 1993-94 and 1994-95, he is perhaps best remembered from his time at Ewood Park for a mid-match altercation with team-mate David Batty. He returned to Chelsea in 1997 and was a member of the side that won the League Cup in 1998, although injuries, particularly during the 1999-2000 season prevented him from adding to his medal tally.

In the summer of 2003, having increased his Chelsea League tally of appearances to 230, he moved to Southampton as part of the £7 million deal that brought Wayne Bridge to Stamford Bridge.

ABOVE Le Saux in action

It was somewhat ironic that the player who had often replaced Graeme in the England side should now do so at club level, but Graeme did have 36 caps to his name.

At the end of the 2004-05 season, with Southampton having suffered relegation from the Premiership, he announced his retirement from playing and has since worked regularly as an erudite television pundit.

Luiz

As recognisable for his silky skill on the ball as his shock of fuzzy curly hair, Brazilian centre-back David Luiz had two successful spells at Chelsea interspersed with a two-year sabbatical at Paris Saint-Germain.

He initially signed for the Blues on deadline day in January 2011 from Benfica and became a key member of the Chelsea team which won the Champions League and FA Cup in 2012, as well as the Europa League a year later.

A 6ft 2in centre-back who could cover either full back positions, or a roaming berth in midfield, he was supremely confident in possession which compensated for his occasional defensive waywardness although his walkabouts did eventually become less frequent.

The Brazilian defender's crowning moment in his first spell with the club was the Champions League Final against Bayern Munich in 2012, where he played with an uncharacteristic discipline and scored the second penalty in the shoot-out.

After nearly 150 games for the Blues, it was surprising that the club let him go although PSG had offered £50 million for the player – then a world record for a defender. He helped PSG secure the domestic Treble two seasons in a row and he was twice named in the Ligue 1 Team of the Year before making a surprising switch back to West London.

The feeling amongst the fans was that Luiz had been deemed not good enough for the first team two years previously so why bring him back? But he proved the sceptics wrong and as a central figure in Conte's new back three, Luiz showed a new maturity as the season progressed.

It was testament to his resilience that he continued to play so well for the rest of the campaign despite nursing a lingering knee injury sustained in a brutal challenge by Man City's Sergio Aguero in December. He played 33 of the 38 games as he won his first Premier League title and was named in the PFA Team of the Season.

The frustrating knee injury ruled him out for much of the disappointing 2017/18 campaign but he came back strongly the following season partnering Toni Rudiger in central defence as Maurizio Sarri switched to a back four and he helped the club win the Europa league.

When Lampard was appointed manager in the summer of 2019, Luiz was again somewhat surprisingly transferred to Arsenal fuelling rumours that he and Lamps were not bosom buddies, although an £8m fee for a 32 year-old was seen as good business.

BELOW David Luiz winning the Europa League final in 2019

Makelele

Sometimes you don't appreciate the worth of a player until he is out of the team or transferred. Claude Makelele was one such player whose defensive skills in front of the defence were pivotal to Chelsea winning two Premier League titles. His dominance in this area was so impressive that the fans have since called it the "Makelele" role even though he is now long gone.

Born in Kinshasa on 18 February 1973, Claude began his career with Brest before switching to Nantes in 1992. Over the course of the next five seasons he enjoyed considerable success, helping Nantes to the French title and reach the Champions League semi-finals.

In 1997, having made 169 appearances for the club and scoring nine goals, the defensive midfielder was sold to rivals Marseille. Claude made just 33 appearances for Marseille before moving to Spain and joining Celta Vigo in 1998, re-establishing his reputation and earning a subsequent move to Real Madrid in 2000.

A member of the side that won the Spanish League and Champions League in 2002, Claude enjoyed three successful seasons in Madrid before a £16.6 million transfer brought him to Chelsea in 2003.

He soon became a regular within the side and at the end of the 2004-05 season had won a League championship medal in a third country. He scored his first-ever goal for Chelsea with a penalty in the last minute of the last home game of the season against Charlton.

ABOVE Hey Makelele!

The 2007-08 season was a period of renaissance for the 35-year-old Makelele, as he played in the majority of Chelsea's fixtures and was instrumental in the club's run to the Champions League Final. He left at the end of the season on a free transfer to see out the remainder of his career at Paris St Germain. He is retired from international football after 71 caps for France whose fans miss him as much as the Chelsea faithful.

ABOVE Juan Mata taking on Jerome Boateng in the 2012 Champions League Final

Mata

For a player to win the Player of the Year Award in both full seasons that he played at the club shows that Juan Mata was some player and a great favourite with the fans.

That Jose Mourinho preferred Oscar in his position as he offered more defensive cover was the main reason that he was transferred to Manchester United in January 2014 for a fee of £37.1 million, as there was no faulting his finishing or his assists in helping team-mates score goals.

A graduate of Real Madrid's youth team, Mata joined Valencia in 2007-08 and became an integral part of the club's midfield, making 174 appearances over the course of four seasons. In August 2011, Mata signed for the Blues for a fee believed to be in the region of 28 million, and in his debut season was part of the team that won the Champions League and the FA Cup. The following year, Chelsea won the Europa League making Mata and Spanish team-mate Fernando Torres the first players to hold the Champions League, Europa League, World Cup and European Cup simultaneously.

Matic

Chelsea could have saved themselves some £20 million if they are kept hold of Nemanja Matic the first time that they signed him.

He first joined the club from MSK Kosice in 2009 for a meagre £1.5 million fee but failed to make an impression and was sold to Benfica as part of the deal which saw David Luiz join Chelsea in January 2011.

Under manager Jorge Jesus, he was converted from a playmaker to a defensive midfielder and his general play so improved Chelsea re-signed him in January 2014. The left-footed Serbian international continued to shine at Chelsea protecting the defence but also launching attacks with his brand of quick, incisive passing. He helped the club win the Premier League title at a stroll and was named in the PFA Premier League Team of the Year.

Speaking to Chelsea TV, the midfielder who played in all but two of the 38 league games said: " We showed this season that we have good character and a good squad and we deserved to be champions. The most important thing is that most of the players are young and this team can improve."

Matic also spoke about the contrast between the 2014-15 season and 2009-10 when he made a contribution to the previous Premier League win. " It is different because I played almost every game this season and in 2010 I only played in three games. I feel I really gave something to this team this season and I am really happy because of that." In July 2017, he was reunited with former Chelsea manager Jose Mourinho after signing for Manchester United which was viewed as something of a shock at the time but arguably the Blues had the best years out of him as he has struggled to make a mark at Old Trafford.

ABOVE Matic having a rest in an easy match against Arsenal

ABOVE McCreadie gets the better of Leeds

McCreadie

The tough tackling Eddie McCreadie gave exceptional service to Chelsea for many years, both as a player and later as manager.

Signed by Tommy Docherty from East Stirling in April 1962 for a paltry £5,000, he quickly established himself as the first choice left back, injuries permitting.

Over the course of the next 11 years McCreadie made 331 League appearances for the club, adding a further 79 appearances in major cup competitions, netting four League goals.

It was his ability to help keep goals out, however, that earned Eddie his place in Chelsea folklore, helping the club win the League Cup in 1965, the FA Cup in 1970 and the European Cup Winners' Cup a year later.

He was equally revered in Scotland, winning a total of 23 caps for his country, including the infamous 3-2 win over then World champions England in 1967.

McCreadie took over from Ron Stuart as Chelsea manager in 1975 when Stuart moved up to General Manager and remained in charge for two years. During his second year in charge Chelsea won promotion back into the First Division and McCreadie, a firm favourite of the fans, seemed set to guide the club back to the glory days. Unfortunately the euphoria surrounding promotion had barely had time to settle when McCreadie left the club, resigning on 1 July 1977 over unacceptable terms offered by the board to continue as manager. He recalled: "Just pulling on the famous blue Chelsea jersey was a thrill indeed. I loved the club and I still love it. It was the most wonderful 16 years of my life."

Mikel

The arrival of John Mikel Obi in the summer of 2006 confirmed Chelsea's determination to add exciting young talent as well as established stars to a squad that had just won back-to-back league titles.

As a junior Mikel had played as an attacking midfielder, but upon moving to West London Jose Mourinho quickly outlined his desire to play the Nigerian in the holding midfield role vacated by Makele, a position he has operated in ever since. A tall, strong upright player, Mikel is tactically astute, moving the ball quickly on to his more attacking-minded team-mates. If he has a failing it is that he has only scored five goals in 334 appearances but the fans have learned to savour them like solar eclipses.

ABOVE John Obi Mikel never one to venture forward

Mikel has won a host of honours during his time at the club, but perhaps his finest moment in a Chelsea shirt was the 2012 Champions League final, when he produced an outstanding midfield display as the team beat Bayern Munich on their home pitch in Germany.

" I have always appreciated the Chelsea fans, they've been amazing. They're always there to support the team week in, week out, which just shows how brilliant they are.

"It's been an amazing journey. I've enjoyed every bit of it. I've worked with some great people, great players from when I came to the ones that are here now. They've all been brilliant."

Mourinho

RIGHT Mourinho deep in thought at a press conference

Indisputably the greatest manager in the history of the club, there is no doubt that Chelsea would not be the major force that they are today without the influence of Jose Mourinho.

He announced his arrival at Chelsea by describing himself as the "Special One" and went on to prove that his team were also special in winning two Premier Leagues, two League Cups, and an FA Cup under his command.

His only failure was his inability to win the Champions League, a feat he had already achieved at Porto. He ran out of time at Chelsea after a bust up with owner Roman Abramovich and left the club by "mutual consent" in September 2007.

Born in Setubal, Portugal on 26 January 1963, Jose Mario dos Santos Mourinho Felix, to give him his full name, is one of only a handful of managers to have achieved greatness without having excelled as a player.

His father was a professional goalkeeper, but despite having spells with minor League clubs, Jose made more of a mark on the management and coaching side of the game, producing dossiers and match reports from which his father's teams benefited.

A degree in sports coaching was followed by a spell as a high school coach and finally a move into higher level football with Vitoria Setubal during the early 1990s.

He then linked up with English coach Bobby Robson when he was appointed coach at Sporting Lisbon, becoming his translator (which earned him the nickname Translator, although

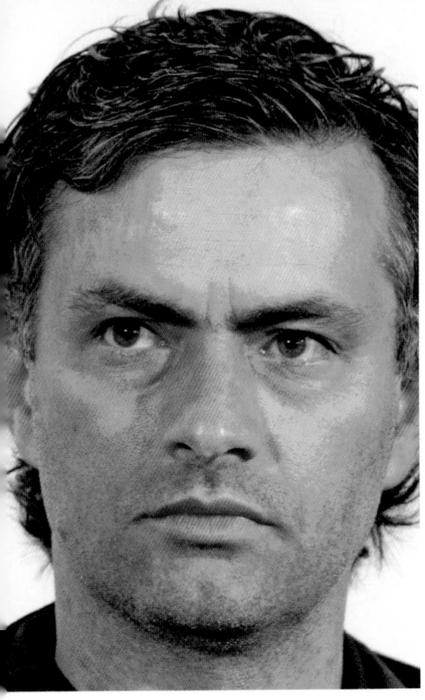

technically he was employed as an interpreter).

He followed Robson to both FC Porto and then to Spain with Barcelona, where he learned the Catalan language. When Robson returned to PSV Eindhoven, Mourinho remained at Barcelona and worked alongside Louis Van Gaal.

It soon became apparent that having to translate and interpret instructions from learned football coaches such as Robson and Van Gaal had awoken coaching abilities in Mourinho, and after expanding his role at Barcelona to such an extent he was contributing to coaching and tactic sessions, he was soon looking for a position of his own. It came in 2000 when he was offered the chance of replacing Jupp Heynckes at Benfica, but after just nine games in

BELOW Jose Mourinho poses with his children Zuca (L) and Matilde (R) and the Premiership Trophy

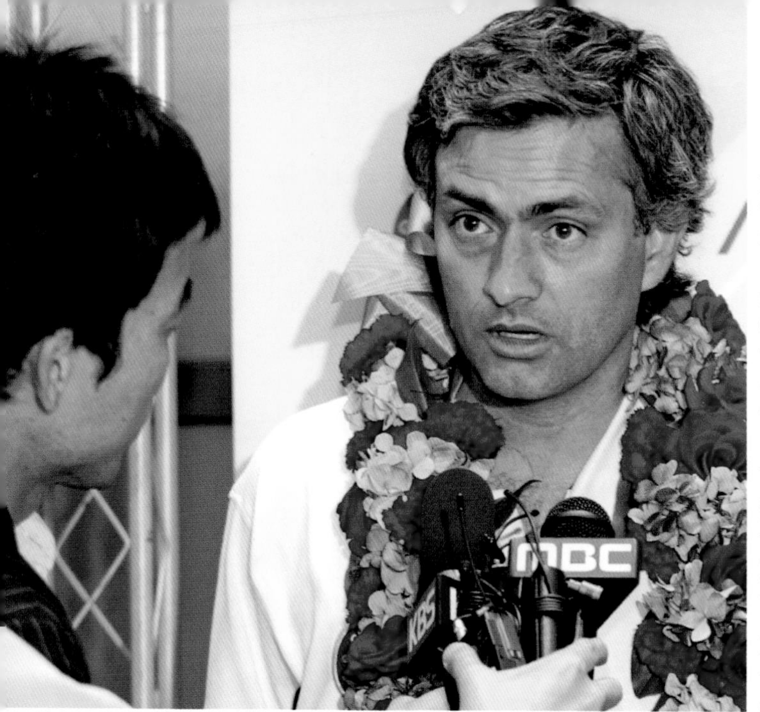

promising he would make them League champions the following season.

His impact was immediate, for at the end of the 2001-02 he had lifted them to third place in the table and qualification for the UEFA Cup.

The 2002-03 season saw the realisation of his promise, for they won the Portuguese League (the Super Liga) by eleven points from Benfica, had won the Portuguese Cup (beating another former club Leiria in the final) and had won the UEFA Cup for good measure, beating Celtic in that final.

ABOVE Mourinho receives a warm welcome in South Korea

charge he resigned when the in-coming President announced he had another coach to take over.

A brief spell at Uniao de Leiria was followed by his appointment as coach at FC Porto in January 2002.

Although the club was languishing in mid-table, was out of contention for the League and faced an uphill struggle to even qualify for Europe, Mourinho was confident of his own abilities,

They repeated their Super Liga success in 2003-04 (albeit with a reduced eight point advantage) and narrowly missed out on the Portuguese Cup, beaten by Benfica for once.

However, there was plenty of compensation to be found in Europe, winning the UEFA Champions League 3-0 against Monaco having previously seen off the likes of Manchester United. Despite or perhaps because of this European success,

MOURINHO

LEFT Back at the helm in his Championship winning side of 2015

Mourinho was soon being courted by most of Europe's top sides and eventually settled on a move to Chelsea, taking over the reins in June 2004.

Although he inherited a top class side from Claudio Ranieri, Mourinho soon identified areas for improvement and brought in almost a new backroom staff and set about turning Ranieri's nearly men into champions.

Mourinho left as the most successful manager in Chelsea's history having won five trophies for the club in three years. He was also undefeated in all home League games.

He went on, in June 2008, to manage Inter Milan where he won a unique treble - Serie A, Coppa Italia and Champions League - and then in 2010 on to Real Madrid where he won the Copa del Ray in his first season. Lured back to the team that had always been his first love in June 2013, Mourinho went through a transitional season in 2013-14 until he had recruited the likes of Costa and Fabregas to the team which went on to win the Premier League at a canter. He won another League Cup but was dismissed in December 2015 after a poor run of results and a souring of his relationship with Eden Hazard and just about everyone else. He was appointed manager of Manchester United and won the Europa League and League Cup in his first season but became more and more miserable as the team's fortunes waned and he was dismissed in December 2018 mid-way through his third season at the club.

BELOW Mourinho's relationship with his best player Eden Hazard turned sour towards the end of his second spell at the club

Nevin

RIGHT Pat Nevin showing perfect balance

BELOW Portrait of Pat Nevin

Pat Nevin remains one of the most exciting players to have pulled on the blue shirt of Chelsea.

Spotted by Clyde playing minor League football in 1981, his performances in the less frenetic Scottish League soon had scouts from south of the border tracking his progress and in July 1983 he was sold to Chelsea.

His impact at Stamford Bridge was immediate, making 38 appearances and scoring four goals in Chelsea's Second Division Championship winning season, earning himself the supporters' 'Player of the Year' award (he would repeat the success in 1987) as well as the accolade of the 'most outstanding player in the Second Division.'

He excelled at the higher level as well, helping Chelsea establish their credentials in the First Division and collecting the first of his 28 caps for Scotland.

In July 1988, after five years and 193 League appearances with Chelsea, he was surprisingly sold to Everton and proved as firm a fans' favourite at Goodison Park as he had at Stamford Bridge.

He was to enjoy three and a half years at Everton, making 109 appearances before being loaned to Tranmere Rovers. The move to Prenton Park became permanent in August 1992 and he would go on to rack up just over 200 League appearances for Tranmere before moving back north of the border and turning out for a variety of clubs.

Pat was almost unique among professional footballers during the 1980s, for whilst most of his contemporaries would cite the likes of Phil Collins and Lionel Richie as their favourite musicians, Pat's invariably came straight from the pages of New Musical Express and he was often a guest reviewer for the magazine.

He was equally up to date with political matters; he may have played on the right wing but his politics came from the left!

LEFT Pat Nevin is the holder of an arts degree

Osgood

LEFT Peter Osgood

The King of Stamford Bridge, Peter Osgood was one of the greatest goal-scorers in Chelsea's history, having netted 150 goals during his two spells with the club.

Initially signed as a junior Osgood was upgraded to the professional ranks in September 1964 and made his debut the same season, scoring twice in a League Cup tie as Chelsea progressed to win the tournament. Initially seen as the ideal cover for Barry Bridges, Osgood made a proper breakthrough during the 1965-66 season until a broken leg brought his career to a temporary halt.

He recovered and emerged to lead the line in his own right, scoring in every round as Chelsea won the FA Cup in 1970, one of only nine men to have achieved the feat.

He netted in both the final and replay of the European Cup Winners Cup the following season, enabling Chelsea to add a further trophy to their record. For good measure, Osgood scored in a final for the third consecutive season in 1971-72, but this time Chelsea lost the League Cup 2-1 to Stoke City.

Osgood remained at Stamford Bridge until March 1974 when he moved on to Southampton, having made 369 League and Cup appearances for the Blues and scored 148 goals.

He remained at The Dell until 1977, apart from a brief period on loan to Norwich City, and left the club with another FA Cup winners medal in his pocket after Southampton had surprisingly beaten Manchester United in 1976.

BELOW Ron Harris (left) and Peter Osgood lift the FA Cup after beating Leeds United 2-1 in the FA Cup Final replay at Old Trafford

After a brief spell in America with Philadelphia Osgood returned to Stamford Bridge to finish his playing career, registering a further ten appearances and two goals.

A member of the England 1970 World Cup squad Osgood won four full caps having already represented the country at youth and Under-23 level. He later worked at Stamford Bridge as one of the greeting legends at home matches. He was only 59 when he collapsed and died at a family funeral on March 1, 2006.

BELOW The King rules

Pates

LEFT Colin Pates

Colin Pates signed apprentice forms with Chelsea straight from school and was upgraded to the professional ranks in July 1979.

He made his debut soon after, appearing in the Second Division match against Orient in November 1979 and over the next nine years would go on to make a total of 281 League appearances for the club, along with more than 50 in various cup competitions. Such was the consistency and reliability of Colin at the heart of Chelsea's defence, only one of his League appearances was as a substitute, an astonishing figure for a man often at the heart of the action.

A member of the side that won the Second Division championship in 1984, the closest he came to a major honour was a winners medal in the much maligned Full Members Cup in 1986, but as the final was played at Wembley, there is no doubt that the occasion is still warmly remembered in the Pates household.

In October 1988 he was sold to Charlton Athletic, going on to make 38 appearances for the club (again with only one substitute's appearance) before moving to North London and Arsenal. Used more sparingly at Highbury than previously in his career, Colin's final tally of 21 appearances included nine as substitute, and in March 1991 he was sent on loan to Brighton & Hove Albion for 17 appearances.

His move to the south coast became permanent in August 1993 and he finished his career with the club, making a further 50 appearances before retiring from playing.

Pedro

A talented two-footed winger, Pedro arrived at Stamford Bridge with a fantastic pedigree having already enjoyed success at the highest club and international levels which he added to as a Blues player.

He made a scoring debut away at West Bromwich Albion in August 2015 and maintained consistent form in his maiden season despite the disruptive mid-term departure of the manager finishing joint-third highest scorer with eight goals from 40 appearances.

In October 2016, he scored the fastest goal of that season when netting after 30 seconds of a 4-0 win over Manchester United in his 50th Chelsea appearance. Pedro's fine form frequently won him selection ahead of the previous season's Player of the Year Willian, at either left wing-back and a right wing-back. The Spaniard scored nine league goals en route to picking up his first trophy in England.

BELOW Pedro has a trophy haul to rival anyone in the game

Pedro's 2017/18 season didn't hit the same heights as the one before, as a switch in formation to 3-5-2 meant he was often forced to try and make an impact off the bench. He did score twice in the FA Cup run though, crucially heading the winner during extra-time of a tight quarter-final tie at Leicester.

Ahead of the 2018/19 campaign Pedro signed a one-year contract extension but he sometimes looked ill at ease with Sarri-ball although the team eventually finished third and qualified for the Champions League.

Pedro excelled in the Europa League scoring twice at home to Slavia Prague in the quarter-finals as well as an important precise leveller in the semi-final first leg away to Eintracht Frankfurt. He was at it again in the final in Baku, converting the second goal with his left foot and finishing the season a Europa League winner for the first time.

If his illustrious club career wasn't enough, he is also one of very few players to have won both the World Cup and European Championships, a feat achieved with Spain in 2010 and 2012 respectively.

Pitch Owners

Chelsea Pitch Owners is an independent organisation that took out a substantial loan to purchase the freehold of the stadium and the name Chelsea FC. The purpose of CPO is to give fans the opportunity to buy a small number of shares in the company that owns the freehold of the pitch. This will ensure that if the developers ever looked to buy the land, regardless of how much it was worth, the shareholders could vote down any such motion.

The share capital of the company is not listed or traded on any stock exchange neither is there any intention to list the share capital of the company upon any investment exchange.

Therefore CPO shares do not increase or decrease in value. But it does help ensure that no one, now or in the future will develop the Bridge into anything other than one of the best stadiums in Europe in which to watch The Blues!

ABOVE Stamford the Lion entertains at the protected Stamford Bridge

RIGHT 1988 Player of the Year Tony Dorigo

FAR RIGHT 1978 Player of the Year Micky Droy

BELOW LEFT 1974 Player of the Year Gary Locke

BELOW RIGHT 1986 Player of the Year Eddie Niedzwiecki

Player of the Year

Official Chelsea Player of the Year List

1967	Peter Bonetti	1976	Ray Wilkins
1968	Charlie Cooke	1977	Ray Wilkins
1969	David Webb	1978	Micky Droy
1970	John Hollins	1979	Tommy Langley
1971	John Hollins	1980	Clive Walker
1972	David Webb	1981	Petar Borota
1973	Peter Osgood	1982	Mike Fillery
1974	Gary Locke	1983	Joey Jones
1975	Charlie Cooke	1984	Pat Nevin

1985	David Speedie
1986	Eddie Niedzwiecki
1987	Pat Nevin
1988	Tony Dorigo
1989	Graham Roberts
1990	Ken Monkou
1991	Andy Townsend
1992	Paul Elliott
1993	Frank Sinclair
1994	Steve Clarke
1995	Erland Johnsen
1996	Ruud Gullit
1997	Mark Hughes
1998	Dennis Wise
1999	Gianfranco Zola
2000	Dennis Wise
2001	John Terry
2002	Carlo Cudicini
2003	Gianfranco Zola
2004	Frank Lampard
2005	Frank Lampard
2006	John Terry
2007	Michael Essien
2008	Joe Cole
2009	Frank Lampard
2010	Didier Drogba
2011	Petr Cech
2012	Juan Mata
2013	Juan Mata
2014	Eden Hazard
2015	Eden Hazard
2016	Willian
2017	Eden Hazard
2018	N'Golo Kante
2019	Eden Hazard

RIGHT Joe Cole of Chelsea

BELOW LEFT Frank Lampard of Chelsea

BELOW Juan Mata

Poyet

For a free transfer, Gustavo Poyet made a valuable contribution in his four years at the club.

The Uruguayan midfielder won the hearts of the fans with his goals, his exuberant celebrations and infectious enthusiasm and during his short time at Chelsea helped the club win the FA Cup and the UEFA Cup Winners Cup.

His first season looked to be over after just two months due to a cruel cruciate injury but recovery was rapid enough to score a tie-changing goal in a Cup Winners' Cup semi-final and play in the triumphant final in Stuttgart.

Important goals became a 'Gus' trademark. He netted a UEFA Super Cup winner and the goal that qualified Chelsea for the club's first Champions League campaign, plus both goals in an FA Cup semi-final against Newcastle.

Goals were plentiful too, with 14 scored from midfield in his second season. Had he not missed three months due to an injury inflicted by a bad foul on Boxing Day, many fans believe Chelsea would have won the league.

Manager Gianluca Vialli's decision not to start him in the Champions League defeat against a Barcelona side he knew well from playing in Spain was the beginning of the end and although he scored 12 goals in his only season under Claudio Ranieri, he fell victim to the tinkerman's wish to revamp the squad.

He was sold to Tottenham as a 33-year-old for a staggering £2m and was soon beating his former club in a cup semi-final, dimming his memory in the eyes of some Chelsea fans but 49 goals in 145 appearances was a praiseworthy goal ratio for a magnificent midfielder.

BELOW Gus Poyet was hired by Premier League team Sunderland as manager in 2013

Quickest

ABOVE Roberto Di Matteo scores for Chelsea in the 1997 FA Cup Final

The early goal all Chelsea fans will remember came in the 1997 FA Cup Final when Chelsea beat Middlesbrough 2-0. While they were still taking their seats at Wembley or settling down in front of the telly, Italian midfielder Italian Roberto Di Matteo whacked a long-range shot past Boro's Ben Roberts to register the quickest goal in the fixture's long history. The official clock timed it at just 43 seconds.

But even champions can slip up as Chelsea did by letting Southampton's James Beattie's score the quickest goal of the Premiership season in 12 seconds for Southampton at the Bridge on 28 August 2004. Joe Cole was the culprit, conceding possession to set up the first goal conceded under Jose Mourinho. The strike was just two seconds slower than Ledley King's fastest ever Premiership goal in 2000. Unfortunately for Beattie, he then deflected Eidur Gudjohnsen's back-header into his own net to cancel out the lead, and Chelsea eventually won 2-1 to ensure a four-game winning streak became five.

As if to show they hadn't learned their lesson, the Blues then went to the Millennium Stadium for the Carling (League) Cup Final in February 2005 and let Liverpool score the quickest goal in League Cup final history after just 45 seconds. They did it again in the FA Cup Final of 2009 against Everton when Louis Saha scored the quickest ever final goal at the new Wembley stadium after just 25 seconds, breaking Di Matteo's record from 1997. Fortunately, the Blues won both matches against the Scouser teams proving the age-old maxim, it ain't over until the fat lady sings!

Ramires

Ramires will always live in the hearts and minds of Chelsea fans for the subliminal chip over Victor Valdes, the Barcelona keeper in the away leg of the Champions League semi-final which saw the Blues reach the final.

What made this goal even more memorable was that Ramires had been booked twice in the tie and would miss the historic game which Chelsea won against Bayern Munich..

Ramires had joined Chelsea in the summer of 2010 for 22 million Euros after one season with Benfica where he was renowned for his quick, direct tough-tackling, yet also for his ability to score high quality goals.

His combative, box-to-box style of play has endeared him to managers and supporters alike, and he is now played more than 200 games for the Blues winning the Premier League, FA Cup, Football League Cup and Champions League.

Ramires featured at both the 2010 and 2014 World Cups for Brazil and has half a century of caps.

His combative, box-to-box of play endeared him to managers and supporters alike, and he went on to play nearly 250 games for Chelsea winning five different domestic and European competitions and Goal of the Season awards. It was surprising when in January 2016 he signed for Jiangsu Suning for £25 million as many fans thought he still had a role to play for the team.

RIGHT Ramirez celebrating the Champions League win with Brazilian and Chelsea team-mate David Luiz

Ranieri

Claudio Ranieri spent his playing days with AS Roma, Catanzaro and Catania. At the end of his playing career he turned to coaching and then management, accepting his first managerial role with Campania.

After two years he moved on to Cagliari, taking the club into Serie A inside two years following successive promotions. His reputation enhanced, he then moved on to Napoli and subsequently Fiorentina in 1993.

It was at Fiorentina that he began to enjoy success, guiding the club to Italian Cup and Super Cup victories. Following this success he switched to Spain, taking over at Valencia and winning the Spanish Cup in 1998 and later guiding them into the Champions League for the first time. Ranieri then accepted an offer to join Atletico Madrid, but wrangles with his chairman meant it was an uphill struggle and Atletico were relegated from the Spanish top flight.

After six months out of the game Ranieri accepted an invitation to take over at Stamford Bridge in 2000, replacing the recently sacked Gianluca Vialli.

His early days at Chelsea were also a struggle, with Vialli being very much a fans' favourite.

Ranieri's stock wasn't helped by his inability to speak English, a situation not helped by the appointment of an interpreter who struggled with Italian and the printing of the manager's notes in the matchday programme in pidgin English!

Added to this was his constant changing of the team both before and during matches, with all three substitutions often taking place at once, which led many to question his tactical abilities. Slowly Ranieri won everyone around, reaching the FA Cup final in 2002 and finding a way of getting the best out of the players he had, especially as there wasn't any money to buy new ones at the start of the 2002-03 season.

He managed to qualify for the following season's Champions League and, with the arrival of Roman Abramovich, suddenly had almost

ABOVE Ranieri: Practise what you preach

RIGHT The Roman army General

unlimited funds available for team strengthening – he spent some £130 million during the course of the season.

As the months progressed speculation grew that Ranieri's position as first team coach was under threat and only the delivery of a major trophy would save his job.

Despite the mounting pressure Ranieri retained his calm, winning over countless fans both inside and outside the club with the assured way he went about his business.

A stunning victory over Arsenal in the Champions League quarter-finals left him on the brink of delivering the greatest club prize of them all, but just as he had done at the beginning of his Chelsea career, he changed the side around at the wrong time.

From drawing away 1-1 against a Monaco side down to ten men, the second leg side lacked cohesion and leadership and slumped to a 3-1 defeat. It was too much of a mountain for the second half and Chelsea went out of the Champions League in the semi-final.

Ranieri's chances of retaining his position went with them and in May 2004 it was confirmed that he was leaving the club.

Ranieri managed various top teams all over Europe before he shocked the football world when he led Leicester City to their first Premier League title in the 2015-16 season – after the team had been given odds of 5000-1 against winning the title.

ABOVE Ranieri speaks at a press conference

ABOVE Arjen Robben leaves another defender for dead

Robben

For a while during his short but successful stay with Chelsea, the Dutch flyer Arjen Robben was almost unplayable.

His speed and fleetness of foot left defenders in his wake but he was often out of the team through injury and while he won two Premier League medals with the Blues, it was felt that his Chelsea career had not lived up to its full potential.

Robben first came to prominence with Groningen for whom he was Player of the Year for the 2000-01 Eredivisie season. Two years later he

signed for PSV where he became the Netherlands' Young Player of the Year and won an Eredivisie medal.

The following season Robben's signature was pursued by leading English clubs, and after protracted transfer negotiations he joined Chelsea in the 2004 close season.

Though his Chelsea debut was delayed through injury, upon returning to fitness he helped Chelsea to consecutive Premier League titles, and eventually made 105 appearances for the club scoring 19 goals.

After a third season in England which was punctuated by injury, Robben moved to Spanish club Real Madrid for £24 million in August 2007. In his first season in Madrid, Real won the League title, Robben's fourth League title in six years. He moved to Bayern Munich in August 2009 where he won eight Bundesliga titles as well as the Champions League. Robben decided to retire from playing football in July 2019 having also won 96 caps for the Netherlands.

ABOVE LEFT SCORE!

ABOVE Robben holds the Premiership trophy

Sexton

ABOVE RIGHT The directors of Chelsea Football Club including film director Richard Attenborough (seated left) and Dave Sexton (standing right) with the FA Cup

BELOW Chelsea manager Dave Sexton signs autographs for young fans

Dave Sexton was the son of a middleweight boxer but chose football as his own profession, going on to play for Chelmsford City, Luton Town, West Ham United, Leyton Orient, Brighton & Hove Albion and Crystal Palace during his career, helping Brighton win the Third Division championship in 1958. At the end of his playing career Sexton switched to coaching and established a good reputation at Chelsea, Fulham and Arsenal.

In 1965 he returned to Leyton Orient, this time as manager, and two years later returned to Stamford Bridge, replacing the recently departed Tommy Docherty. Whilst Sexton inherited the nucleus of a good side, he bought wisely and constructed a side that could compete for the game's top honours, finally landing the FA Cup and European Cup Winners' Cup in successive seasons.

Chelsea also reached the League Cup Final in 1972 but lost to Stoke City. Sexton then fell out with several important players, such as Peter Osgood and Alan Hudson who were subsequently sold. This, combined with other problems at the club, ensured that Sexton didn't come close to repeating his earlier success and he was sacked after a poor start to the 1974-75 season.

Shortly afterwards, he was appointed manager of Queens Park Rangers. With a team containing the likes of Stan Bowles and Gerry Francis, as well as players recruited from ex-club Chelsea, John Hollins and David Webb, Sexton took Rangers to within a point of the League title in 1975-76. They were top after playing their final game, but Liverpool's late

ABOVE Police keeping back crowds of Chelsea supporters as they strain for a glimpse of manager Dave Sexton

win over Wolves denied them.

He took over at Manchester United – again succeeding Tommy Docherty – but his reign at Old Trafford failed to deliver any trophies and in the pressure atmosphere that was engulfing United, Sexton seemed an inevitable casualty. The highlight was an FA Cup Final appearance in 1979, losing 3-2 to Arsenal in a dramatic match, and finishing as League runners-up to Liverpool in 1979-80. Sexton was dismissed in April 1981, despite having won his final seven games in charge, and managed Coventry City for two years (preserving their top flight status) before leaving in 1983 to go into semi-retirement.

Whilst that remains his last full time management role, Sexton has been in demand for his coaching knowledge, assisting the England set up under Bobby Robson and later Sven Goran Eriksson, setting up a scouting network for the latter.

The first Technical Director of the FA National School at Lilleshall, Dave Sexton OBE still retains his affection for Chelsea, citing his FA Cup triumph of 1970 as the most memorable of his career. For guiding Chelsea to the first sustained success in their history, Chelsea fans retain their affection for Dave Sexton too.

RIGHT Frank Sinclair celebrates scoring his goal against Real Betis

BELOW Sinclair-borne

Sinclair

Frank Sinclair began his Stamford Bridge career as a trainee and was upgraded to the professional ranks in 1989.

He made his League debut the following year and remained with the club for almost ten years, making 169 League appearances and scoring seven goals (for Chelsea). He also had a spell on loan at West Bromwich during this period, making six appearances for the Baggies during the 1991-92 season.

A member of the side that won the FA Cup in 1997 he missed out on the Cup Winners Cup the following year and moved on to Leicester City during the summer of 1998.

He was to enjoy six seasons with the Foxes before moving on to Turf Moor and Burnley.

A Jamaican international with 24 full caps to his name, Frank had, prior to joining Leicester City, registered 11 goals for his then three clubs.

He is perhaps more famous for the number of own goals he has scored, all of which seem to be spectacular efforts that would have been worthy of being scored at the correct end!

LEFT Speedie celebrates a goal with striking partner Kerry Dixon (right) and defender Joey Jones

BELOW David Speedie

Speedie

David Speedie was a feisty and much travelled forward who gave great service to 11 clubs during the course of his career.

Signed as a junior by Barnsley he was promoted to the professional ranks in October 1978 and made a total of 23 appearances for the Yorkshire club, although he was unable to score.

He was sold to Darlington in June 1980 and, in a lower division, began to establish himself as a proven goalscorer, netting 21 goals in 88 appearances before being snapped up by Chelsea.

He arrived at Stamford Bridge in June 1982 and would ultimately form a lethal strike partnership with Kerry Dixon, who arrived a year later.

Over the course of five seasons Speedie scored 47 goals in 162 appearances, but just as his partnership with Kerry was beginning to reap real dividends he was sold to an ambitious Coventry City and made his debut for the club in the FA Charity Shield at Wembley.

He went on to make 122 appearances (netting 31 goals) for the Sky Blues before being surprisingly transferred to Liverpool in February 1991.

Playing in a more deep lying midfield position, Speedie was unable to make a real impact at Anfield and was soon on his travels once again, joining Blackburn Rovers in August 1991. Nearly a year later he was sold to Southampton and later had spells at Birmingham City, West Bromwich Albion and West Ham United before finishing his career with Leicester City.

He made ten appearances for Scotland, the last coming in 1989.

Stamford Bridge

BELOW Chelsea playing at Stamford Bridge in 1919

Stamford Bridge is somewhat unique among the major grounds, for whilst the likes of Old Trafford and Highbury were built to suit the needs of Manchester United and Arsenal respectively, Chelsea was formed to fill an existing ground!

The site that now houses Chelsea FC originally opening on 28 April 1877 as the home of the London Athletic Club and was used for athletics only.

In 1896 brothers HA (Gus) and JT Mears tried to buy the leasehold of the site, finally succeeding in 1904 following the death of the previous owner (a Mr Stunt) and the expiry of a clause in the original contract that gave the London Athletics Club two years grace after the death of the owner.

The Mears brothers finally got control of the site in September 1904 but even then were not convinced that a football club was the best way of filling the ground on a more regular basis. There was an exceptional offer on the table from the Great Western Railway Company that seemed closest to success (and would give the brothers

a more than sizeable return on their investment) but tentative enquiries were made as to whether Fulham, the only other local side, would be interested in moving into Stamford Bridge, a plot that offered more potential than Craven Cottage.

Fulham turned them down, preferring to remain at the Cottage, which left only the prospect of Stamford Bridge becoming a coal dumping yard for the Great Western Railway.

Fate, or rather a dog, then took a hand; at a meeting with Gus Mears, friend Frederick Parker tried to convince Gus Mears that the ground could become a viable alternative to Crystal Palace, then the venue for the FA Cup final, which would realise a potential profit of £3,000 a game.

Mears was unconvinced until Mr Parker's dog bit him on the leg, and Gus Mears was so taken with the cool manner in which Mr Parker reacted, he reckoned he could trust his judgement on the fate of Stamford Bridge!

Whilst others set about building a side, Gus Mears and Frederick Parker concentrated on building a ground suitable. Impressed with what they saw in Glasgow, they employed architect Archibald Leitch to do the designs. His plan was simplicity itself, with a main stand (the East Stand) and banking around the other three sides to create a natural bowl.

It was originally intended that Stamford Bridge would accommodate 95,000 (most of them would have been without cover) but this figure was tested only once.

It was, however, the second biggest ground after Crystal Palace but it was not until after the First World War

BELOW Stamford Bridge in 1969 covered in a blanket of snow

ABOVE The magnificent Stamford Bridge as it looked in 2005

that Stamford Bridge got to host an FA Cup final, and then only for three years. Fears that Chelsea might reach the final and play on their own ground were heightened in 1920 when Chelsea made the semi-final, and by 1923 the FA had settled on a new and neutral venue for all future finals, Wembley Stadium. Stamford Bridge itself developed little until 1930 when the Shed End terrace and cover was erected, along with a greyhound track around the pitch!

For the next 40 or so years Stamford Bridge changed very little, although bits seemingly were added here and there and there was no real uniform design to the stadium.

That was to change in 1973 with the first phase in what was planned to be the construction of a new Stamford Bridge, capable of accommodating 50,000 fans in an all-seater circular stadium.

The East Stand was the first to be built, an impressive three tier stand that towered over the rest of the ground, but the cost of building the stand virtually

bankrupted the club and meant the rest of the plans remained unfulfilled.

With the club in such massive debt ownership of the ground passed out of their hands and there were fears for almost ten years that the club would have to consider moving elsewhere, but eventually ownership was won back in 1992 and two years later new and revised expansion plans were put into place.

The North Stand, built with funding from Matthew Harding and renamed in his honour following his death, was the first phase in a new circular style stadium, but this time the stands were nearer the pitch, generating a better atmosphere.

The Shed End was rebuilt in 1997, complete with the Chelsea Village Hotel, to generate additional income for the club, and in 1998 the final piece of the jigsaw, the West Stand, started. Problems over planning permission meant that the upper tier was not completed until three years later, but when finished lifted the capacity at Stamford Bridge to 42,449, all under cover.

The Chelsea Village complex also features two four star hotels, five restaurants, conference and banqueting facilities, a nightclub, health club and business centre.

ABOVE Stamford Bridge

BELOW A waterlogged pitch at Stamford Bridge in 1998, not quite all under cover yet

Tambling

ABOVE RIGHT Tambling tries a shot
BELOW Bobby dazzler!

Bobby Tambling was spotted by Chelsea whilst playing for East Hampshire Schools and was taken on as an apprentice in July 1957 and upgraded to the professional ranks in September 1958.

He scored on his League debut for the club in February 1959 but it was to take the departure of Jimmy Greaves before Tamblingwas able to establish himself as a regular in the side.

Thereafter he was a prolific goalscorer, netting a Chelsea record of 164 League goals over the course of 302 appearances, including a record–equalling five in one match against Aston Villa in September 1966. A member of the side that won the League Cup in 1965 he also helped the club reach the FA Cup Final in 1967, netting Chelsea's goal in the 2-1 defeat by Spurs.

Unfortunately for Tambling, by the time Chelsea had re-assembled a side to challenge and win major honours his career at Stamford Bridge had started to falter, hampered by injuries and he was loaned to Crystal Palace in January 1970.

The move became permanent during the summer, with Palace paying £40,000 to secure his services, and over the next three years Tambling made 68 League appearances and scored 12 goals. He wound down his playing career in Ireland, having spells with Cork Celtic (where he also served as a player-manager), Waterford and Shamrock Rovers before finally retiring.

Capped for England at schoolboy and Under 23 level, Bobby also won three full caps, netting one goal.

Terry

Captain, leader, legend ... John Terry is the most successful player in Chelsea's history who captained the club more than any other player.

He picked up his first winners' medal in 2000 and his last in 2017. His final trophy was a fifth Premier League and 15th major honour overall. He left the club he joined as a 14-year-old having made 717 appearances - a figure topped only by Ron Harris and Peter Bonetti – scoring 67 goals before having swansong seasons as a player and coach at Aston Villa.

JT made his debut in October 1998 and by the first full season of the next century he had established himself in Claudio Ranieri's side alongside seasoned international stars such as Marcel Desailly and Frank Leboeuf.

His tactical awareness and leadership qualities earned him the captaincy for the first time in December 2001, a couple of days before his 21st birthday. He would go on to skipper the side more than 500 times, easily a Chelsea record.

In the summer of 2003, after Terry's consistent form at the heart of the defence helped the club secure Champions League football, he made his first senior England appearance. He would later captain the Three Lions and feature at two World Cups and two European Championships notching 76 caps.

ABOVE John Terry lifts the FA Cup in 2007

ABOVE Yet another Terry tackl

He ensured his place in the hearts of all true Blues fans after he bravely stepped up to take a penalty in the Champions League Final against Manchester United in 2008 (one that should have been taken by Drogba who had been sent off) and slipped and missed denying Chelsea the trophy for the first time in their history.

He eventually got his hands on the Champions League trophy in 2012 (although he didn't actually play in the Final due to suspension) and a Europa League trophy the following year meant that he had a full set of medals. He won the FA Cup five times and the League Cup on three occasions.

Arguably his best individual season was in 2004/05 when Mourinho made him permanent captain. The team conceded just 15 goals on its way to their first league title in half a century, and as a result JT was named the PFA Player of the Year.

JT's last appearance came on an emotional day at Stamford Bridge when he was substituted in the 26th minute of the final home match against Sunderland – the same number as he had worn on his shirt throughout his Chelsea career.

ABOVE Chelsea celebrate winning the FA Premier League once again in 2006

The Trophy Cabinet

Trophy	Years
League Title	1955, 2005, 2006, 2010, 2015, 2017
FA Cup	1970, 1997, 2000, 2007, 2009, 2010, 2012, 2018
Champions League	2012
Europa League	2013, 2019
Cup Winners Cup	1971, 1998
Super Cup	1998
Community Shield	1955, 2000, 2005, 2006, 2007, 2009
League Cup Winners	1965, 1998, 2005, 2007, 2015
Old League Division Two Winners (now called 'The Championship')	1984, 1989
Full Members/ZDS Cup Winners	1986, 1990
FA Youth Cup Winners	1960, 1961, 2010, 2012, 2014, 2015
UEFA Youth League	2015

Three Hundred Club

Player	Dates played	Apps	Goals
Ron Harris	(1961-80)	795	14
Peter Bonetti	(1959-79)	729	–
John Terry	(1998-2017)	717	67
Frank Lampard	(2001-2014)	648	211
John Hollins	(1963-75) & (1983-84)	592	64
Petr Cech	(2004 - 2015)	494	0
Dennis Wise	(1990-2001)	445	76
Steve Clarke	(1987-98)	421	10
Eddie McCreadie	(1962-74)	410	5
John Bumstead	(1976-91)	409	44
Ken Armstrong	(1946-57)	402	30

BELOW The 1972-73 Chelsea squad, featuring captain Ron Harris (back row, third from right) and Peter Bonetti (back row, fourth from left), who have made the most and second most appearances for Chelsea

Player	Dates played	Apps	Goals
Didier Drogba	(2004-2012) (2014-2015)	381	164
Peter Osgood	(1964-74) & (1978-79)	380	150
Branislav Ivanovic	(2008-2017)	377	34
Charlie Cooke	(1966-72) & (1974-78)	373	30
John Obi Mikel	(2006-2017)	372	6
George Smith	(1921-32)	370	–
Bobby Tambling	(1958-70)	370	202
Roy Bentley	(1948-1956)	367	150
John Harris	(1945-1956)	364	14
Harold Miller	(1923-39)	363	44
Eden Hazard	(2012-2019)	352	110
Frank Blunstone	(1953-64)	347	54
Colin Pates	(1979-1988)	346	10
Marvin Hinton	(1963-76)	344	4
Peter Houseman	(1962-75)	343	39
Ashley Cole	(2006-2014)	338	7
Jack Harrow	(1911-1926)	334	5
Tommy Law	(1925-39)	319	19
Gary Locke	(1972-82)	317	4
Micky Droy	(1970-85)	313	19
Graeme Le Saux	(1987-93) & (1997-03)	312	16
Gianfranco Zola	(1996-2003)	312	80
Jackie Crawford	(1923-34)	308	27
Bobby McNeil	(1914-27)	307	32

ABOVE Tommy Law (right) shakes hands with Sam Weaver. Tommy made 319 appearances for Chelsea

ABOVE Torres playing for Chelsea as a second half substitute in the Champions League Final 2012

Torres

For a player whose career at Chelsea was deemed a failure, Fernando Torres might say that it wasn't as bad as people made out as he won three major trophies including the Champions League.

Torres started his career with Atlético Madrid making his first team debut in 2001 and finished his time at the club having scored 75 goals in 174 La Liga appearances. His form prompted a big money move to Liverpool in 2007 for a club record transfer fee. He repaid this in spades by becoming the fastest player in the club's history to score 50 league goals.

Having scored 81 goals in just 142 appearances, Torres left the club in January 2011 to join Chelsea for a British record transfer fee of £50 million. In his first full season at Chelsea, Torres won the FA Cup and the Champions League although his goal-scoring prowess had dipped alarmingly. The following season he scored in the Europa League final helping Chelsea to win the competition for the first time.

But injuries had cost him that crucial extra yard of pace and his confidence in front of goal was fragile. After just 45 goals in 172 appearances, the club loaned him out to Milan and then sold him back to his home town club Atletico. For all his critics, his CV boasts a roster of trophies including three major international tournaments, Euro 2008 and 2012 and the World Cup 2010. He has been capped 110 times by Spain and is his country's third highest goal scorer with 38 goals.

Under-rated

BELOW Under-rated Brazilian? Alex made just 68 appearances in three seasons at Stamford Bridge

With big name players holding every position at Chelsea few of today's players can consider themselves under-rated. But some can still claim to have not been given a fair crack of the whip - perhaps they did not get an extended run in the team or were played out of position.

Take Lassana Diarra, for example, who played only a handful of games for Chelsea and then went on to Real Madrid where he earned rave reviews as a holding midfield player; and, to some extent, Glen Johnson who had a stuttering stint at right full-back and after leaving the club became a regular in the 2010 World Cup squad as well as the most expensive full-back in the Premier League when he signed for Liverpool for £17 million in June 2009.

Players of the past who tended to be overlooked by the press (if not the fans) in favour of their superstar team-mates include Peter 'Mary' Houseman, a left

ABOVE Marco Ambrosio

RIGHT Dave Beasant

winger/midfielder who laid on goals for the likes of Osgood and Hutchinson in the late 1960s/early 1970s, and whole-hearted Welsh defender Joey Jones who starred in the early 1980s.

More recently who can forget the 2004 heroics of fourth-choice goalkeeper Marco Ambrosio as Chelsea left Highbury with a 2-1 Champions League victory. Wayne Bridge wrote the headlines with the deciding goal four minutes from time, but it was the underrated keeper's heroics that ensured the home team were restricted to a single goal. And talking of keepers, Dave Beasant was shipped out by Ian Porterfield when he suffered a 'mare' against Norwich in 1992 – yet would continue to play professionally into his mid forties. His manager, by contrast, failed to see out the season…

In terms of underrated Chelsea teams, one candidate is John Neal's mid-1980s side which included the likes of Kerry Dixon, Pat Nevin and Mickey Thomas. But after 2005's glorious campaign, Chelsea are unlikely ever to be under-rated again!

Some fans might argue that Maurizio Sarri was under-rated as a manager, as although he only lasted one season, he finished third in the league and won the Europa League final before returning back to Italy to manage Juventus.

Vialli

Gianluca Vialli is one of only a handful of men who have both played for and managed Chelsea, combining both positions for a period towards the end of the 1990s.

Gianluca Vialli is one of only a handful of men to have both played for and managed Chelsea, combining both positions for a period towards the end of the 1990s.

He began his career with the local Cremonese club and made just over 100 appearances before a switch to Serie A with Sampdoria.

By the time he came to England in 1996, he had also played for Juventus and won every domestic and European honour available, including two Serie

A titles (one for each club), four Italian Cups, the UEFA Cup, the European Cup Winners' Cup and the UEFA Champions League, captaining

BELOW Gianluca Vialli in action

ABOVE Chelsea manager Gianluca Vialli and Dennis Wise lift FA Charity Shield, 2000

ABOVE RIGHT A portrait of Vialli

Juventus in the 1996 final.

A few days later a free transfer saw him join the growing foreign revolution at Stamford Bridge and join compatriot Gianfranco Zola. His impact was immediate, finishing the 1996-97 season as Chelsea's top goalscorer and had collected a winners medal in the FA Cup (he replaced Gianfranco Zola some 12 minutes before the end of the match).

However, Gianluca's greater contribution was being felt in the dressing room, and when Ruud Gullit was sensationally sacked in February 1998, Gianluca was immediately offered the position of player-manager.

The following month he led the club to victory in the Coca Cola League Cup (although he didn't play) and two months after that victory in the European Cup Winners' Cup (in which he did). In May 2000 came further glories in the FA Cup, but it was to be something of a swansong for Gianluca.

Having spent some £57 million on players since his appointment, rumours of dressing room unrest were the last thing the club needed and in September 2000 he was sacked.

He eventually resurfaced as manager of Watford, but without the same kind of resources his tenure did not last long and he has since appeared on television as a pundit. Despite the circumstances surrounding his removal, Gianluca presided over a time of sustained success, something the club had been striving for over decades.

Walker

ABOVE Walker of Chelsea goes in for a tackle against Ossie Ardiles of Spurs

Winger Clive Walker joined Chelsea as an apprentice and moved up to the professional ranks in April 1975.

It took him a couple of years to make a regular breakthrough into the side but when called upon he usually turned in dazzling performances, none more so than in 1977 when Chelsea beat Liverpool, then reigning European champions 4-2 in an FA Cup tie at Stamford Bridge, with Clive contributing two of the goals. Although he made 224 appearances for the club in his nine years, he struggled to shake off the tag of super-sub, even though the facts were somewhat different; he only made 33 appearances as a substitute.

However, as his introduction from the bench usually coincided with an upturn in Chelsea's performance, perhaps it was a moniker well earned.

Clive left Chelsea in July 1984 with their First Division status being reclaimed and having netted 60 League goals during his time at Stamford Bridge, and would later give equally good service to Queens Park Rangers, Fulham and Brighton where he finished his playing career. He later became a television pundit.

ABOVE David Webb clears the danger

Webb

David Webb was an amateur with West Ham United before moving to Leyton Orient to begin his professional career. He spent nearly three years with the club before moving to the South coast to join Southampton and over the next two years developed into one of the best full backs in the country.

Chelsea signed him in February 1968 and over the course of the next six years he became a vital member of the side. David's Chelsea career is perhaps best summed up by two matches against the same opposition, Leeds United in the FA Cup final of 1970. In the first match, playing a strict full back role he was given a torrid time by Eddie Gray, being constantly beaten by the trickery of the Scottish winger.

At the end of the match, which finished a 2-2 draw, both Chelsea in general and David in particular looked as though they had achieved an unlikely reprieve. In the second match manager Dave Sexton switched things around, handling responsibility for marking Gray to Ron Harris and moving David into a more central defensive role.

Whilst Gray's threat was blunted by Harris, David thrived on the space and freedom he now had and in extra time it was he who headed in the winning goal.

The following season he was an

equally vital member of the side that won the European Cup Winners' Cup against Real Madrid.

He proved his versatility to Chelsea in December 1971 when, with Peter Bonetti, John Phillips and Steve Sherwood all injured, he played against Ipswich Town in goal! Remarkably, after dropping to his knees and praying in front of the Shed, he helped the Blues keep a clean sheet in a 2-0 victory! David remained at Stamford Bridge until July 1974 when he left to join Queens Park Rangers, subsequently playing for Leicester City, Derby County, Bournemouth and Torquay United before retiring as a player in 1984.

He then became manager of Torquay and also had three spells in charge at Southend United. He was also briefly manager at Stamford Bridge, answering a crisis call from the club in 1993 with a brief to conduct an audit of the playing staff during his spell in charge.

It was widely believed that Webb would benefit from the audit but, although he did a good job in his few months in charge, Glenn Hoddle was subsequently lured from Swindon to take over control.

BELOW Webb fights for the high ball

ABOVE Ray Wilkins with Graham Rix

ABOVE RIGHT Ray Wilkins watches from the dugout

Wilkins

Ray Wilkins was an excellent servant to the club both as a dynamic midfield player and part of the management team under Carlo Ancelotti.

Nicknamed Butch during his childhood, he joined Chelsea as an apprentice and rose through the ranks to make his debut against Norwich City in October 1973.

It was the 1974-75 season that saw him become established as a permanent fixture in Chelsea's midfield, progressing to become captain of the side at just 19 years of age, the youngest captain in the club's history. This was despite the presence of several older, more experienced players on the club's books; Wilkin's ability to appear calm and composed when all around him was mayhem (such was the nature of Chelsea's play at this period) was an inspiration to his teammates.

It was also said that his play showed a certain negativity, with Wilkins often playing the square sideways pass rather than looking forward earning him the additional nickname of The Crab. Despite suffering relegation under his captaincy Chelsea bounced back and Wilkins' reputation soared with it, culminating in an £800,000 transfer to Manchester United in August 1979.

Wikins was with United for five years, helping them win the 1983 FA Cup (his only domestic honour) before a move to AC Milan for £1.5 million in 1984 where he found his true vocation. First capped for England in 1976 against Italy, he won 84 caps over the next ten years, captaining his country on ten occasions and scoring three goals.

After a long playing career (including 84 caps for England) Wilkins moved into coaching and was twice assistant manager at Chelsea, under Gianluca Vialli from 1999 to 2000, and from September 2008 to November 2010, under Luiz Felipe Scolari, Guus Hiddink and Carlo Ancelotti.

The football world was shocked when he died of a heart attack on April 4 2018 at the age of 61. During Chelsea's home game against West Ham a few days later, fans at Stamford Bridget gave a minute's applause in the eighth minute and held a banner which read: "Ray was one those select few, he knew what it meant to be one of us a real blue blood. Chelsea flowed through his veins, may you rest in peace Ray."

BELOW Brothers Graham (left) and Ray ('Butch') Wilkins

Willian

RIGHT Willian training with the Brazilian team

Chelsea fans knew what they were getting when the Blues bought Willian after seeing him score twice in a virtuoso display for Shakhtar Donetsk at the Bridge in 2012.

The Brazilian signed a five-year contract in August 2013 having moved to England from the Russian club Anzhi Makhachkala. Although regulations state that non-European players must be regular internationals, Willian was given a work permit despite only having two caps at the time, as an FA panel deemed that were he not Brazilian he would be a regular.

Comfortable operating in any of the three attacking midfield positions behind the main striker, Willian is quick, robust and creative in possession. As his first couple of Chelsea goals proved, he also has an eye for the spectacular when it comes to the art of scoring.

He was chosen to play for Brazil in the 2014 World Cup when he came on for his club-mate Oscar in a match against Chile in which he missed a penalty in the shoot-out, although Brazil still went through.

In the Champions League game at Qarabag in November 2017, Willian made his 200th Chelsea appearance and marked the occasion by scoring two goals. He should play his 300th game for the club (scoring more than 50 goals) in the 2019/20 season and with the transfer of Hazard, assume the mantle of the main man on the pitch.

Wise

London-born Dennis Wise joined Southampton as an apprentice straight from school but never made the grade at The Dell, being allowed to leave and subsequently joining Wimbledon in March 1985.

He made his debut for The Dons before the season was out but made just four appearances during the 1985-86 season. The following season, Wimbledon's first in the First Division, saw Dennis become something of a regular and the heart, along with Vinnie Jones, of the so-called Crazy Gang.

Dennis was an integral part of the side that won the FA Cup in 1987-88, netting the winner in the semi-final and responsible for crossing the ball over for the only goal of the final.

One of the last of the original Crazy Gang left, Dennis moved on to Chelsea in July 1990 for £1.6 million.

Over the course of the next ten years he gave Chelsea exceptional service, both on and off the pitch, and was the heartbeat and captain of the side that won two FA Cups and the European Cup Winners' Cup.

The higher profile he enjoyed at Chelsea was rewarded with his first cap for England in 1991 and he would go on to win 12 caps for his country, scoring one goal.

In June 2001, after 332 League appearances and 113 games in other competitions (he is fourth in the all-time list of Chelsea appearances), Dennis was allowed to join Leicester City, linking him once again with his former mentor Dave Bassett, but during

ABOVE A Wise move

the summer of 2002, an altercation with a teammate saw him sacked by the club and he subsequently joined Millwall. Later elevated to player-manager, he guided them to their first FA Cup final (Dennis's fifth) in 2004, but at the end of the 2004-05 season he resigned and returned to Southampton, where his career began. In May 2006 he was named player-manager of Swindon Town, with former Chelsea legend Gus Poyet his assistant.

Aside from his efforts on the pitch on behalf of the club, Chelsea fans have good reason to honour Dennis, for along with Ken Bates he galvanised the club as part of the Chelsea Owners club, ultimately ensuring the club's future at Stamford Bridge. He is still fondly remembered in song by fans on most match days for his "******* great goal in the San Siro" equalising in the 1-1 draw with AC Milan on October 26 1999.

RIGHT Jon Harley, Dennis Wise, and John Terry help launch the new Chelsea kit in 2001

X-tra time

ABOVE David Cameron, Barack Obama, Angela Merkel, Jose Manuel Barraso and Francois Hollande watching the penalty shoot-out during the G8 summit

Whilst Chelsea have featured in many matches that have gone into extra time, perhaps the most memorable was in the final of the Champions League in 2012.

Bayern, who were playing on their home pitch, took the lead late in the second half through Thomas Muller but Didier Drogba equalised for Chelsea five minutes later with a flashing header to take the game to extra time, in which Arjen Robben missed a dubiously awarded penalty, Petr Cech saving the low drive. The teams stayed level at 1–1 and the match went to a penalty shoot-out which Chelsea won 4–3 to clinch their first Champions League title. Drogba took the successful spot kick which at that time was his last kick fort the club until he returned for his swan song.

Domestically the FA Cup Finals of 1970 were also as dramatic. The first match at Wembley, on a heavy and energy sapping pitch, had seen Chelsea constantly playing catch-up against Leeds United, equalising for a second time shortly before the end of the allocated 90 minutes.

Extra time was little more than an exercise in survival for both sides, as cramp and strains began to affect the twenty two players out on the pitch.

The replay at Old Trafford seemed set to continue in a similar fashion, with Leeds taking the lead and being pegged back by Peter Osgood's diving header.

This time, however, Chelsea showed the more determination during extra time, creating a number of chances that might have put the match beyond doubt.

As it was, Ian Hutchinson's long throw was flicked on at the near post and David Webb stole in at the back to head home the decisive winner.

Youth Team

RIGHT John Terry, one of Chelsea Youth Team's greatest successes

OPPOSITE Zola in action

Chelsea's youth set-up, or the Academy as it is now known, runs teams from the under- 9s to the under-23s in the hope of unearthing some home grown gems such as Callum Hudson-Odoi which could save the first team millions of pounds in transfer fees.

The academy has won myriad trophies over the years but more importantly has produced great players such as brothers Ron and Allan Harris, Peter Bonetti, Bobby Tambling, Barry Bridges, Bert Murray, John Hollins, Peter Osgood, Ray Wilkins, Graeme Le Saux, Bobby Smith, Terry Venables, Jimmy Graves and captain leader legend John Terry.

Another current notable from the academy is Ruben Loftus-Cheek who has been with Chelsea since the Under-8s age group and is a talented box-to-box midfielder who has already won several full England caps; while Tammy Abraham and Mason Mount, who both joined Chelsea when they were under 10 years-old, are now first team regulars and full England internationals. Despite still being in their early twenties, they are already worth in excess of £50m each – showing the value of the youth team set-up when it is allowed to flourish.

From the 2013-14 season, the development squad play their home games at the Ebb Stadium, home of Aldershot Town FC, while the under-19s & 18s generally play their home matches at the club's Cobham training ground. Both teams occasionally use Stamford Bridge for the big matches.

Zola

Sardinian-born Gianfranco Zola remains the most popular and amongst the most successful of all Chelsea's overseas recruits.

He began his career with the Sardinian club Nuorese in 1984 and later with Torres, finally being spotted and signing for Serie A club Napoli in 1989.

Initially used as something of an understudy to Diego Maradona, Gian-franco helped Napoli win the Italian title in 1990.

The following year he picked up a winners medal in the Italian Super Cup and collected the first of his 35 caps for Italy after being selected by coach Arrigo Sacchi.

In 1993 he moved on to Parma AC and two years later helped them win the UEFA Cup (2-1 on aggregate against fellow Italian

RIGHT Gianfranco Zola shows off his OBE for his services to football

OPPOSITE Gianfranco Zola celebrates scoring

perhaps the only winner to have received the accolade without completing an entire season.

There was better to follow, for the following season Chelsea won the Coca Cola League Cup and European Cup Winners' Cup, with Gianfranco scoring the only goal of the game against fb Stuttgart. Further success came in the European Super Cup in 1998 and the FA Cup in 2000, the last at the old Wembley.

Zola was regarded as one of the best Italian creative forwards of his generation, and as one of the best players in Premier League history. He was voted by the fans as Chelsea's Greatest ever player.

club Juventus), the Italian Cup and finish runners-up in Serie A, they're highest ever placing.

In November 1996 a £4.5 million fee brought him to Stamford Bridge and had an immediate effect on the club; at the end of the season they had won the FA Cup and Gianfranco had been named Footballer of the Year by the Football Writers' Association,

After retiring from playing, he has not been able to apply his genius to managing or coaching and has had undistinguished stints at West Ham, Watford and Cagliari as well as acting as Maurizio Sarri's sidekick back at Chelsea for the 2018/19 season where he looked baffled at the manager's negative tactics and predictable substitutions.

Fly
Emirates

ABOVE Publisher Jules Gammond wishes bon voyage to Joe Cole who swopped the Blues for the Reds in July 2010

The pictures in this book were provided courtesy of the following:

GETTY IMAGES
101 Bayham Street, London NW1 0AG

PA PHOTOS
paphotos.com

Design and artwork by Alex Young

Published by G2 Entertainment Limited

Publishers Edward Adams and Jules Gammond

In Memory of life-long Blues fan Mo Claridge
31st March 1951 – 25th December 2005